MUSTARD SEEDS AND WATER LINES

MUSTARD SEEDS AND WATER LINES

KAREN MILIOTO

Published by River Birch Writing Co.

ISBN-13: 978-0-9994130-0-5

For Ruth

May you always be anchored by your roots, always value new growth, and never forget the importance of planting good seeds.

Chapter 1

"It is *STILL* raining," I grumbled to Brad as I rolled over in bed and checked the time on my watch. I had woken to the sound of water pouring off our roof and onto the deck below. I was so exhausted, I couldn't trust my body to tell me if it was time to wake up or if it was the middle of the night. My bones said "middle of the night." My clock said "get up."

I closed my eyes and sunk my head into the pillow one last, sweet time, then hoisted myself out of the soft sheets and onto the cold wood floor beneath me. I groaned as I zigzagged my way down the hall and through the maze of cardboard boxes.

Our former home had sat on the market for nearly a year after we'd moved here, an hour north. But it had finally sold, and with the closing date fast approaching, we were scrambling to pack up the stacks of boxes that remained inside its walls and bring them here. In doing so, we were facing the fact that we had purchased a much smaller house than the one we'd left behind. Last night, we had struggled to unload box after box in the dark and the torrential rain. For the life of me, I had no idea where any of it was going to go.

I poured a cup of coffee and began to accept that a rainy day might be just the thing I needed. It was the only force capable of keeping me indoors long enough to address the growing piles of books, trinkets, and memorabilia at my feet.

I heard a loud bang behind me and turned to see Brad jumping up and down, holding his right foot in pain.

"Don't wake up Ruth!" I whispered with a wince.

I wanted to comfort him and his stubbed toe, but not at the expense of waking up a two-year-old who had gone to bed three hours too late last night. No good ever comes from prematurely awoken two-year-olds.

Brad hopped to my side, balancing himself with his hand on my shoulder while he rubbed his now reddish-purple toe. I kissed his cheek and offered him a cup of coffee. Then I peeked into the living room to assess the mass of boxes and get an idea of just how bad my day was going to be.

I didn't even recognize half the stuff we'd moved the night before. Picture frames from 1993. College textbooks I had now moved three times without opening them once in the interim. Maybe today would be the day we drew the line in the sand on some of this stuff for the sake of our sanity and our survival.

"When did you learn to speak Italian?" I asked, lifting a white and red CD set from the top of a Rubbermaid container.

"Senior year of college, maybe?" He walked over to where I was standing and took the box from my hands.

"How did that go for you?" I said. Both of us knew the only word either of us had learned in Italian was *gelato*. Oh, and *cannoli*. Couldn't forget *cannoli*.

He set the CDs down on the coffee table and took a final sip from his mug. Then he headed toward the door.

"Have fun today," he quipped, gesturing toward the disaster.

I watched him pull out of the driveway and then looked at the clock. It would be at least an hour before Ruth woke up, so I pulled on my mud boots, grabbed my raincoat, and headed outside to feed our two horses their breakfast. Our dogs, Olive and Clyde, followed close on my heels as I headed down the long dirt road that led to the barn at the far end of the property.

It felt good to get outdoors, away from the mess of boxes, and to remind myself why we had chosen to move here in the first place. For years, we had said we wanted a small house on a large piece of land, and this spot fit the bill. It was a long, twelve-acre lot, full of towering magnolia trees and regal live oaks delicately draped with wisps of Spanish moss. A rolling hill led to a tiny creek that ambled through the woods and eventually poured into the Amite River. The river was majestic, gravel-bottomed with crystal-clear water flowing past massive white sandy beaches lined with cypress trees. It was like another world, just thirty minutes north of Baton Rouge.

I crossed the creek and studied the branches of a giant oak limb that wrapped up and over the road before me. Its bark was covered in bright green moss, and its leaves glistened in the freshly fallen rain. I could deal with the boxes and limited space. I just needed to remember that with those inconveniences came this road.

As I walked into the barn, I was greeted by the soft nickers of our two horses, Jack and Grady.

"Are you guys bored?" I asked.

I scratched Jack behind the ears and slipped a carrot to Grady. Jack nuzzled my hair, and I set to work measuring their feed and dumping it into their buckets. The rain was loud on the tin roof, and I took my jacket off and hung it on a stack of hay bales while I cleaned and filled their water buckets and dropped piles of hay at their feet. I spread brand-new pine shavings in their freshly cleaned stalls and then leaned on Jack's shoulder for a minute to consider my plans for the weekend.

The barn was a mess, littered with piles of things that had been moved from the seven-stall barn we were leaving at our old home. I had procrastinated on moving everything, knowing I didn't have a good place to put any of it in the two-stall barn we had here. Buckets, hoses, and jump standards were piled everywhere. It stressed me out almost as much as the boxes waiting for me inside the house did. *I just need some time*, I thought, *and some dry weather.* Neither of those were coming easily these days.

Jack nudged his head against my shoulder, and I rubbed his thick neck vigorously. He never tired of attention.

I studied his solid build and shining coat and thought back to the day, six years ago, when I had brought Jack home. He was eight years old then and had just finished his racing career—a "war horse," as those who race long at the track are known. Unfortunately, when I found him, he was a far cry from the horse that had stepped off the track for the last time a few months earlier.

A friend who ran a rescue program at the track had sent me a picture of Jack that had been taken a few days before his retirement. He was majestic. A blanket of perfectly toned muscles covered a quintessentially lanky thoroughbred frame. His eyes were bright, and his dappled bay coat shone under the Louisiana sun.

When I went to see him, that picture in hand, the tattoo on his upper lip was the only thing that convinced me he was the same animal. He was emaciated, with the hair of his coat missing in huge patches from rain rot. There were mats in his mane and tail, and no one had trimmed his feet, so his hooves were twice as long as they should have been. It was painful to watch him walk around on the back of his heels through that muddy paddock.

He was not the horse I needed, nor was he the

one I wanted, but he was not staying at that place for one more minute. With the help of a friend, I loaded him into my horse trailer and busted him out of that nightmare that same day. On the drive home, I renamed him Jack, after my first dog. It felt cleansing in a way—a new name for a new beginning, one in which he would always be taken care of.

"I want to hang with you guys today," I said, standing upright and giving Jack one last scratch, "but it's raining buckets, and I have a mess at the house, so fun will have to wait until tomorrow."

Grady peeked his head over the door as I latched Jack's stall, a giant bunch of hay hanging out of his mouth. I laughed at the expression on his face.

"I'll see you two goofballs later," I called over my shoulder as I left.

When I stepped into the rain, Olive came bounding toward me with a tree branch double her length hanging out of her mouth. She was four months old and thought nothing of clotheslining her human companions with whatever she happened to drag beside her. I jumped out of her way and then reached down to rub Clyde behind his ears as he sauntered beside me, matching my pace.

"You're too old for her games, aren't you, buddy?" I said to him.

He wagged his tail and looked up at me through the rain, his blue eyes shining in agreement.

I typically loved the long walk home from the

barn, but this rain made it tricky. I slipped on the slick clay as I climbed the last hill before the house.

I shook my boots off on the stairs and left them by the door, coated in wet clumps of mud, then studied the growing pile of shoes by the entrance to our kitchen and sighed. If the weather didn't let up soon, we would all run out of dry footwear. Our world was already messy and muddy enough on a sunny day. Rain just amplified matters for us.

When I opened the door, the dogs breezed past me and began rolling their wet coats on the Oriental rug in the center of our living room, their muddy paw prints covering its light tan and green surface. *I give up*, I thought. *We just aren't clean people.*

Taking a seat on the couch, I reached for my coffee mug, then rested my right arm on a box of high school yearbooks and my left arm on an oversized vase that hadn't been used since Valentine's Day 2007. The whole scene would have been moderately funny if it wasn't my stuff and my problem.

Moments later, I heard Ruth calling from her bed. When I opened the bedroom door, she was sitting up, arms outstretched for me to grab her.

"How was your night, baby?" I asked, pulling her into my arms and then balancing her on my left hip before heading back into the kitchen. "What did you dream about?"

"Jacky!" she replied with delight.

I placed her down at the table and poured her a cup of milk.

"We were running *so* fast in the woods," she said. "I was holding so tight to his reins. We were *trail* riding!"

I laughed as I set the cup down in front of her. In the new book I bought her the week before, three young friends set out on their ponies for their first trail ride and proceeded to get lost in the woods. Ruth loved the story, but she was adamant she and Jack would never get lost in the woods. They were a team of two superheroes, after all, and superheroes never get lost.

Ruth crunched on the cereal in front of her, and I turned my attention to the nearest moving box within reach. Three stacks began to form around me: *donate*, *trash*, and *keep*.

A few hours later, I stacked the last box of extra clothes and homewares by the door to be donated, then heard my phone ding with a text message. It was my mother-in-law, checking to see how we were making out with the rain.

Brad was born and raised in a small suburb of New Orleans, and his family grew cautious whenever a weather-related threat came around.

It didn't help that earlier this year, we'd experienced a hundred-year flood in our area and, out of an abundance of caution, had evacuated the horses to higher ground when the creek clogged from backfill off the river. Meteorologists had called the events leading up to that March flood a "perfect storm." They likened it to a weather event in the '80s that had caused historic flooding in our immediate area.

It had started when a storm dropped excessive rain on towns about an hour or two north of us. A few days later, when our rivers crested from the runoff up there, a large system delivered high rain totals locally. It was, essentially, a double flood, with the new rain falling on an already swollen river.

Parts of that day had been nerve-racking, but in the end, it all seemed like a lot of chaos over nothing. The creek did flood, but the water never came close to the barn and receded within hours of rising. I felt a little silly for having made the horses swim across the creek and then sit in the rain all afternoon while their dry barn sat empty.

Our state motto is "Get a game plan" when it comes to hurricanes and other disasters, and I felt confident in mine moving forward. I knew the creek would back up and make it hard to get to the horses when the river flooded, but I also knew they were safe back there. I had marked a tree with the water level and then compared it with all the charts and historical data. I figured out that in the worst possible case recorded, a foot or two of water could get in the barn, but there was a second hill behind it that would still be dry. My game plan was to let the horses loose if it seemed like the creek might rise. Then they could swim across on their own if they wanted or stay on the hill behind the barn.

I looked up from my mother-in-law's text and checked the creek. It was still well within its banks.

"We're good," I texted back. "Thanks for checking on us!"

I loved that people cared enough about us to check in, but this wasn't a hurricane, typhoon, monsoon, double flood, tropical depression, or tropical storm. This was a rainy Friday. I set my phone down, feeling relaxed. I had a game plan.

After lunch, I smiled to myself as I broke down the final cardboard box and stacked it by the door to be recycled. Ruth sat in the middle of the living room surrounded by Legos—a mess I was willing to trade for the peace and quiet they provided.

I turned my efforts toward the kitchen and began emptying and then filling the dishwasher. As I wiped the counters down with a sense of accomplishment, I looked over to see my phone buzzing with a flash-flood warning for our area.

I rolled my eyes as I read the short text and muttered, shaking my head, "Who comes up with this stuff?"

Flash-flood warnings never made sense to me. Where was the science in them? Some days the warnings came through when the sun was shining and we were in the middle of a drought. These alerts were, in my humble and uneducated opinion, the meteorological equivalent of crying wolf. They came too often and never amounted to anything.

I clicked the message closed and ignored it.

As I wiped the last pile of crumbs from the island in the center of the kitchen, I took a moment to survey my finished project. With the exception of the Lego mountain forming in the living room, I was fairly certain this was the cleanest this house had been since we'd lived here. I had a two-year-old, after all. I was always one step behind my dryer and my dishwasher, and I was perpetually trailed by a path of Barbie shoes and puzzle pieces. My house was rarely presentable, much less clean.

Not knowing what to do with my new status as purveyor of clean house, I put Ruth down for her nap and went back down to the barn to check on the boys. It was three o'clock, and the creek had risen a bit, but no alarms were going off in my head. As I walked over the bridge, I noticed the water was not higher than my boots. By the time I got to the barn, you could not see standing water anywhere.

Grady was the first to greet me when I stepped into the timber-framed structure. I opened his stall door and popped in to give him a proper scratch.

An appendix-bred quarter horse who often looked like he had walked off the pages of a magazine and into my pasture, Grady had a personality that sometimes reminded me of an adolescent boy: curious, mischievous, bold, and confident, but still in need of his mama from time to time.

He searched my back pocket for a treat while I rubbed his neck.

"I know you're sick of being rained on, buddy," I said. "I know you have better things to be doing today."

I reached down and smoothed the center of his sleek chest. It was his sweet spot. He stretched his neck and wiggled his nose in appreciation.

As I left, I kissed Jack's nose and rubbed the soft, velvety exterior of his muzzle.

"I promise this won't last forever," I said.

I believed those words were true.

By five o'clock, the creek had noticeably risen. I sent a text to my neighbor Tessa to see if she wanted to come with me to let the horses loose. Ten minutes later, I stepped onto the porch to pull on my boots and saw her ducking down the path between our houses with a raincoat pulled over her head. She had moved in next door a few months earlier, and we had bonded quickly over a similar sense of humor and a shared appreciation for a glass of wine after our kids went to sleep.

"Nice day for a stroll!" I yelled over the thunderous rainfall slamming into the steps that led to my porch.

She laughed, and we set off down the hill together.

We waded through the overflow from my pond, and she motioned to the creek. "I guess this is the price we pay for the river, isn't it?"

"March was worse," I said. "In March, the pond and the creek merged and went all the way to that tree." I pointed toward a big oak that stood about a hundred yards from us. "Luckily, the hill is so high back there, it didn't affect the barn. But we had no idea what to expect, so we brought the horses through and loaded what we could in the boat and then floated it across."

"That is crazy to imagine," she said, steadying herself as we inched across the bridge.

The creek had picked up a current, and I was surprised to find it was tough to keep my balance. My boot got caught in a patch of squishy clay, and I stumbled. I reached for Tessa's shoulder, and we made our way up to firm ground on the other side of the now submerged bridge.

I pointed to the tree where I had marked the highest water line from the March flood. "That's my hundred-year flood marker," I said, noting the thin white string still tied around the base of the leggy gum tree halfway down the hill on which the barn was built.

The horses were excited to see us but confused when we opened their stall doors and encouraged them to come out unrestrained. Grady wavered in the doorway, so I tugged on his thick black mane, urging him out. He wandered about ten feet from the barn and began munching on a patch of overgrown grass.

I looked around and noticed the water was barely

visible from where we stood. Was I overreacting? The water had so far to go before it would pose a threat to the barn, and surely standing in a few inches of water was safer for the horses than their being let loose and liable to run away.

I shook my head, frustrated by my indecision.

Then, studying the woods on all sides of us, I realized either option was fine. The woods were so dense, there was no chance the horses would wander into them with so much fresh grass to enjoy right here. I worried too much, I decided. My game plan was a good plan.

I looked back and saw Jack hesitating to leave the comfortable seclusion of his stall. Grady wasn't above bullying Jack, and the poor little guy didn't look eager to leave his safe zone to spend the night being reminded of his spot in the pecking order.

"You'll be okay, sweet Jack," I hollered from the doorway. I propped his stall door open so he could leave when he felt ready.

"Be sweet to Jacky," I told Grady, patting his rump as we turned toward the house.

When I looked back over my shoulder, I caught a glimpse of Jack standing in the doorway. He had pivoted to watch us go, and I couldn't help but notice how beautiful he was in that moment. His dark bay coat glistened in the rain, and his thick, black, unruly mane lay tousled on his forehead and chunky neck. His ears pricked toward us. He looked baffled by his newfound freedom.

We had only been in the barn about ten minutes, but already the walk back was more difficult. The water over the bridge was deeper, and the current cut through us, making it hard to maneuver.

An hour later, I found myself crouched beside Brad's wood shop with a pair of binoculars, straining to see the outline of the horses through the trees. They were standing next to each other, perfectly still, with water about twenty feet from them.

"What?" I whispered under my breath, wondering if the dusky hour somehow tricked my eyes. I had just been over there. How on earth did it rise that fast?

I set the binoculars down and tilted my head in confusion, squinting as I attempted to process what I had seen.

We had to go get them. Something wasn't right.

A short while later, I texted Tessa, asking if she would keep an ear out for sleeping Ruth. Then I watched as Brad launched the boat into the overflowing banks of our pond. It had been less than two hours since we'd returned from our trip to the barn, but at this point, walking was no longer an option.

I grabbed Brad's hand and hoisted myself into the olive-green hull of our twenty-foot flat-bottomed fishing boat. I wondered if I was overreacting in the same way I had in March—the way I had vowed not to repeat. Still, I knew I would sleep better if Jack and Grady were close to me when night fell.

Brad started the trolling motor and pointed us toward the other side of the creek. The boat lurched forward, and I shivered a little in the pouring rain. *Why are we doing this*? I wondered. Surely I was making too much of this. We had already seen this property in a flood. We knew it would be okay. Why couldn't I trust my game plan?

I sat in the boat, my steel seat wet and slippery. My soaked jacket hung heavily on my shoulders. The cold rain penetrated my body, and I realized Jack would be covered in rain rot within days if I didn't treat his coat soon. I'd need to head to the feed store in the morning and get some spray.

I reached for my phone to type myself a reminder note but then realized it wasn't in my pocket. I looked back at the house and noticed we were much farther from it than I expected. Why were we still on the boat? Shouldn't we have been walking by now?

While my mind had wandered into the details of wet hoofs, rain rot, and equine bubble baths, we had driven our boat well beyond the bank of our creek—the same creek I had walked beside just two hours earlier.

I started to feel uneasy. Things weren't right. There was too much water. Our boat was struggling to navigate the overflow that was filling up our pasture on the other side.

We slammed into a tree. I grabbed the pole we

use to maneuver through the shallow marshes of the Gulf during fishing trips and used it to push us off. The trolling motor wasn't cutting it with the current whipping through on all sides of us.

My brain felt foggy. Who needs a hundred-and-fifty-horsepower motor to get past a tiny flooded creek?

I watched the fence posts and noticed them going underwater. With every post we passed, it made less and less sense. None of them should have been underwater.

My mind couldn't process the magnitude of the flooding while helping Brad keep the boat on the right track. It had been ten minutes, and he had not been able to get the motor to start. With each unsuccessful turn of the key, the current rolled us closer and closer to the woods. We were stopped by a big oak tree, which caused the boat to get pinned between the strength of the tree and the power of the water.

We pushed against the tree with every ounce of strength we had in order to get the boat unlocked, but the wet bark ripped at my hands, making it impossible to get a grip. The tree and the water were too strong for us.

We were failing.

Brad grabbed me and pulled me toward the back of the hull, which shifted the weight in the boat and dislodged us. As the boat spun around the tree, we locked eyes, knowing things had almost come to an end for us.

But there was no time to consider that point further. We were still stuck out there, with no life jackets and no phones in a boat that wouldn't start.

I gazed up the hill toward the barn and squinted through the rain. The horses stood next to the barn, about knee-deep in water. Jack was pacing a little. Grady stood stoic.

I wanted to jump out and swim to them.

The motor still wasn't starting, and we were getting pulled farther and farther off course by the current.

I started praying out loud. "Lord, please start this boat. You have to start this boat."

The stormy weather made the sky dark earlier than it should have been, and the rain beat down on us. Every second we sat there, we were wasting precious time and valuable daylight.

At this point, I wasn't even thinking about how we were going to get back to the house. I just knew I had to get to the horses.

I prayed again, this time louder. I was almost yelling at God. I needed Him. "Lord, please start this boat!"

My desperation grew with each futile attempt. It felt like the storm and the night were about to swallow us whole—until, finally, the motor started.

Relief spread over my body. "Thank You, Lord!" I cried.

We made it the rest of the way but startled the horses with the loud motor, and they took off.

Water flowed through the barn. We floated into the center aisle, and I jumped off to get a halter and lead rope for each horse.

The current shot me away the moment I got out of the boat, and I was lucky to get my hand on a stall door to stop myself from being washed away with every other thing that had been in the barn. We needed life vests, but who brings life vests to their backyard?

Brad lifted me back on board the boat, the cold, hard frame of which was slippery yet comforting after my run-in with the current.

The horses were huddled past the barn, in a corner along the outside of my fence line. We tried to approach them quietly, limited by the fact that walking was out of the question and they were skeptical of the boat. Water streamed around them like a pier in the middle of a channel. They were nuzzling and softly grooming each other. Grady's gentle manner toward Jack was so uncharacteristic that it made me lose my cool. They didn't think they were going to make it, and that made me doubt it too.

I looked at Brad with tears in my eyes, but he was determined. We would get them. This would be fine.

It was getting tough to see with the growing dark, but the flashlights scared the horses, so we had to let the moon guide us. The muted light of the moon softened the dark night sky and cast a bluish hue on it through the clouds. I had never seen anything like it.

We used the boat to herd them back into the barn and into one stall. In the safety of the stall, Brad was able to walk up to the horses through the water without getting knocked off his feet. I remember watching him, in awe of how undeterred he was. His jaw was set, and he moved with such confidence and ease, despite the insanity of the situation. His body language alone conveyed to me we were all getting out of there. Things were going to be okay. If we could just get the horses' leads on them, this would all be over and we could all escape this nightmare together.

But in the few fleeting minutes we were in the barn, the water closed in on us. I looked up and noticed the boat quickly reaching the rafters—the same rafters that had caught my eye countless times before, when I had thrown my head back, laughing at something Ruth had said. This building had been our secret getaway, the place I came to dream, to relax, and to watch Ruth indulge in the nature surrounding us.

No doubt all of the coloring books, markers, and jars of paint that haphazardly decorated the barn floor were gone. Ruth's leaf collection, her buckets of pinecones and sticks—all of it would have floated somewhere in the dark abyss of water that had engulfed us.

Chills ran down my back as I watched the water bobbing like waves in a busy harbor.

"We have to get out of here," I finally said, the words leaving my mouth as soon as the thought reached my mind.

For the first time, I grasped the reality of what was happening. This was more than a nightmare. We were—all of us—minutes away from getting trapped and dying in that barn.

I started to think about Ruth, at home and sleeping in her bed. She needed us to get back to her that night. I looked around and realized we were fighting for our lives just as much as we were fighting for the horses' lives—and it was a battle we weren't guaranteed to win.

The issue wasn't that we were moving too slowly. It was that the water was moving way too fast. If we failed to keep ahead of the rate it was rising, then we would join the countless items being swept into the woods on all sides of us.

Grady was willing and ready to follow as soon as Brad secured his halter. It was as if he remembered what had happened in March and understood the strange and noisy vehicle was going to get him out of this growing mess. He came right out of the stall and waited for us to get him to dry land. I promised him we would get him to dry land.

Jack was nervous, though. It reminded me of what I had been taught about barn fires as a child. Horses are not always willing to leave what they believe is the comfort of their stables, and sometimes they refuse to follow their rescuers out. People have died trying to convince terrified horses to come with them.

I understood all of this and could see the correlation, but I wasn't willing to leave Jack. I had promised him years ago he would never be mistreated again, and I intended to follow through on that promise. I also knew the place he had in my little girl's heart. He was Ruth's cherished companion. Her best friend. The hero and the prince in all her fairy tales. She needed me to fight for him. She would have fought for him if she could.

"Jacky, you have to fight, boy," I said, rubbing his jaw softly. "You have to trust me. We are going to get you out of here, but you need come with us."

Tears began to roll down my cheeks as Jack stood anchored in place, terrified.

The water was gaining on us, and I knew we were running out of time.

"Fight!" I cried, wishing I could fight for him, wishing I could budge his twelve-hundred-pound frame.

Finally he mustered the courage to follow. But the moment he was no longer braced by the side of the barn, the current swept him straight into the fence. Then his leg caught in the adjoining fence, which was completely submerged.

Three times, we leaned into the water, current flying, and lifted his body off the wire fence. I held his head and rocked it while his legs thrashed. I watched as his beautiful brown eyes filled with fear.

At some point, the water whisked all of us over the fence and into the wood line on the other side of the barn. Suddenly, everything I had loved about this place was threatening to kill us. The boat was lodged in the very trees whose beauty I had reveled in countless times before. The Spanish moss fell into the boat as it rammed into the trees the moss had once draped. The thick woods made it impossible to reclaim my horses from the rushing tide. The solitude I had cherished left us to fight this battle alone in the dark, with no hope of rescue.

"Where's Grady?" Brad asked, looking up from his attempt to dislodge a now motionless Jack from the trees.

I shook my head, tears pouring down my face. A red welt cut across the palm of my hand where Grady's lead rope had been a moment before.

He was gone. Lost in the pitch-black night.

I looked around and realized the weight of all the hope that had sustained us just moments before had been washed away. I didn't even have the option to keep fighting for them. I was out of options.

I wondered at that moment, as I watched the water pour around us, if this was how we were going to die.

I was scared to set off on the relentless ride across the pasture again. I didn't want to hit any more trees. I was terrified the boat might nearly flip again. I never wanted to feel the rush of the current slamming into my body again. I didn't trust the boat wouldn't break and leave us stranded in this place that used to be my home but now looked more like the set of one of Hollywood's most terrifying movies.

I was out of fight.

Had it not been for the little girl in pink unicorn pajamas who slept back at the house, blissfully unaware of the nightmare unfolding on all sides of her, I would have shut down completely. Everything in me was immobilized by fear. I was physically, emotionally, and mentally depleted, and I wasn't sure we would survive the trip back to our house.

We had no choice but to try, though.

I sat, defeated, in my seat—the same seat that had carried me through countless fishing trips along the marshy Louisiana coastline. A seat I had once loved in a life that had once been filled with joy. I felt every ounce of happiness draining out of my soul, leaving me emotionless and empty.

A quarter of the way home, the prop got tangled in the electric top wire of the fence. The boat came to an abrupt halt, and I sat and considered the possibility that this could be it for us. I watched as Brad methodically unwrapped each long foot of wire tape. The hull swung with the current and tightened the grip he was working so diligently to loosen.

He finally broke us free from the tangled fence, and we were on our way. I was soaking wet and freezing cold but didn't feel I deserved to be anything but that. I wanted to believe this was a dream and that we would wake up from it. But as I looked around my world, so familiar but so dark, I knew I would not be so lucky.

I watched the light from the back porch as it slowly came into focus and led us home. I felt torn between the urge to run toward the house to solidify we were okay and had made it back alive, and the desire to stay anchored in the boat, refusing to accept the defeat that had been handed to us at the barn. I wanted to celebrate our homecoming, knowing our fate could have been so different, but I didn't feel I deserved to have survived at all.

The boat lurched to a halt as it hit the side of the hill in our backyard. I stepped out and stumbled, my legs shaky. The ground felt strange—solid, compared to the hours I'd spent tossed in the boat, but not as solid as it once felt. Nothing was solid anymore.

We walked inside, and I stood, dripping wet, on our tiled kitchen floor. I looked around. Everything was exactly as I had left it. My phone sat on the counter. Ruth's dinner was on the stove. I turned on the video monitor and saw her snuggled in her bed. The contrast between the world we had just left and our tidy home seemed so drastic, it hurt.

I climbed into bed knowing I wouldn't be able to sleep. My mind couldn't escape the images that were now burned into it. I sat up the entire night, shaking and watching the water slowly creep up on our house. We were not sure when, if ever, it would stop. I wanted Ruth to wake up needing me, as she so often did in the middle of the night. I wanted to hold her and know nothing was going to rip her from my arms.

That night, the world was a weird and evil place in which nothing was off limits or sacred. Nothing could be assumed or trusted. No one was safe.

Chapter 2

One week later, I sat with Tessa, watching the kids play on the now dry grass. The two of us were all but motionless in our seats as we looked out over the pond.

I hadn't slept or laughed in seven days. The week behind us was a blur. Tessa had been gutting houses all week. Brad and I had bounced around, cooking for people without kitchens, dropping off supplies where they were needed, and even sandbagging the house of some dear friends downriver.

There was no end in sight to the chaos.

I stared at the grass as it bent and swayed with the movement of the kids' feet. It felt strange to see grass pushing up from the murky brown water so soon. Why did the water get to go? It should have stayed long enough for its victims to wrap their heads around the devastation it had created.

Instead, the water came and left like a tornado. The sun came out the next day, and dry land was thrust back on us like a swift slap in the face by a passing stranger, the aggressor no longer present to be held accountable for our grief.

The kids giggled and squealed, but Tessa and I shared a comforting silence. It left me free to replay scenes from the week in my head like clips from a movie.

The first morning, the sun had risen, exposing water as far as we could see. The meteorologists all but gave up on forecasting the river's next move. One storm chaser woke up in a flooded hotel and turned to social media to urge anyone in the water's vicinity to get out while they still could.

The mood across our area was to run away, but it was too late for our family. We had nowhere to go. Our only option would have been to get back in the boat to battle the water once again, and I couldn't begin to think about doing that. I didn't know if I would ever willingly get into a boat again, much less a boat in that swift water.

Worse than all of that was the idea of putting Ruth into any situation that resembled the night before. Instead I sat, insistent on anchoring my family in our home, refusing to acknowledge the floodwater steadily gaining on us. I watched as it bobbed on our back-porch steps. I saw the roof of our workshop slowly disappear in the murky brown tide. I studied the massive expanse of water and willed the horses to appear from it somehow.

I carried Ruth's tiny purple life vest with me everywhere I went that first day, unsure in each new moment that passed if the water would surge again, sending us fleeing its path. I couldn't trust that water. It didn't follow any rules.

Now, sitting in our backyard six days later, I

couldn't shake the feeling of that merciless water gaining on me again. I watched as our kids chased each other with delight and couldn't help but wonder how easily the tables could have turned and left them all motherless. Tessa and I had walked back to the barn without a care in the world one hour before it started to rise at breakneck speed. What if the water had come half an hour earlier? What if we'd been back there on foot when it pushed through and rose four and then five and then six feet? We could have been stuck, with no way to let anyone know—or, worse yet, we could have walked onto that flooded bridge without realizing how strong the current was and been whisked away before either of us knew what was happening. That whole afternoon and evening, the sky was dark. Between that and the torrential rain, we could barely see. We would have just stepped right into it and been gone, ripped off our feet and out of the lives of those five young children.

Goose bumps formed on my arms at the thought of that and every other near miss we had somehow survived in those horrible hours.

I shook my head and turned my eyes toward Ruth, who was sitting in the middle of the yard, stacking the few sand toys we had recovered from the woods and then knocking them down with delight. She was so sweet and smart. She should have woken up that Saturday morning to her daddy being off work and pancakes cooking in a cast-iron skillet. Instead she was confronted with vanished pets and her home surrounded by water.

Tears welled up in my eyes as I thought about how she sat on the living room floor that first evening, surrounded by Legos and building a barn with walls six stories high.

"Why so tall?" I asked.

She looked up at me, focused and intent, and said, "To keep the water out."

My two-year-old was building flood walls with shiny, multicolored blocks.

On the third day, the water had receded slightly, but our cell phone service was down. We ventured out of the confines of our home in search of a landline to contact our worried parents.

The reality that met us on that first journey out of the house was bleak. Suddenly, our tragedy became the tragedy of every single person in our town. Our story was just one of hundreds of thousands laced with heartbreak and terror.

The reel of images in my head sped up as I pictured the snapshots of chaos we encountered on that first drive. The gold sedan, abandoned in the middle of our street, its doors open wide. It faced the wrong direction and sat partially in the ditch, water dripping from its interior. No doubt that car held a story of survival, or at least I hoped.

A few feet down, we found an eighteen-wheeler

on its side, blocking the road almost entirely. As we slipped past the narrow opening left between its bumper and the curb, we met a small herd of young cattle standing, bewildered, in the street.

The deeper we traveled into the mess, the faster the images played back through my mind. The boats tied to telephone poles. The people in canoes rescuing pets from attics. The lines of cars in the center of town, abandoned with broken windows. A fire truck on its side in a ditch.

Our town and the lives of everyone around us, in ruins.

I shook my head when the reel of memories got too heavy and too fast for my heart. There was too much wrong.

"I think we need wine," I said, standing up to head into the house.

"Please," Tessa replied, without looking up.

"Mommy, I need to go with you!" Ruth cried. "Mommy, don't leave me!"

She shot up from her spot in the middle of the yard with tears pouring from her eyes and a face nearly purple with anguish. I stared at her in shock. She loved to play with Tessa's kids. She'd been excited to get outside and run. She never cared when I left a room.

I started to say something but then remembered that things had changed for my little girl that week.

She had kissed two of her most precious companions goodnight, and they weren't waiting for her when she woke up again. They were lost at sea, or so it seemed. Her soul was justifiably insecure.

I picked her up and balanced her on my hip as I headed into the house, tears burning my tired eyes.

A few minutes later, I came back out, producing a bottle of red wine and two glasses. I poured a bit into each glass and sat down again, resuming the shared silence with Tessa.

I swirled the wine gently in my glass. As my wrist moved through the motion, I couldn't help but notice my mobility suffering under the weight of things. My shoulders were tense and hollow, and I could follow the sensation down my arms and legs. I wondered when I would find the courage to move back into the world again. I was becoming paralyzed.

I glanced over my right shoulder, knowing what was out there, past our fence line and down our road. More of the torment, more of the sadness, more of the loss.

Sunday afternoon had been the first day I left the house without Brad, and I almost didn't make it down the driveway. In the seat next to me sat Ruth's life preserver, a pair of scissors, and a hammer. There weren't enough tools or safety devices to convince me I could venture out with confidence. I hesitated at the end of the driveway, the car sitting in reverse, my hand not ready to put it in drive.

Just as I considered turning back toward the house, I looked in the rearview mirror and saw Ruth studying me, waiting to see what my next move would be.

Brave or defeated?

I had to try to be brave. At the very least, I had to *pretend* to be brave.

I pulled out and headed south down our road. Together, Ruth and I scanned each and every field in search of Jack and Grady. Twice I pulled over, convinced I had seen them, but faster than I could roll down the window, I realized none of them were ours. Our horses had vanished.

About two miles from our house, I ventured down a side street and stopped to talk with some people who were pulled over on the side of the road, searching the woods for someone or something of their own. I recognized the eldest man in the bunch. He was probably around eighty, and Brad had often joked that the man was my boyfriend because I would get excited when we drove by his farm and he was working cattle from the back of a horse at his ripe old age.

As if his lifestyle wasn't awe-inspiring enough, his house was breathtaking. It was a large white mansion that would have been quite at home on the cover of *Southern Living*. It had a shiny tin roof with a huge staircase that led to an enormous wraparound porch.

The property was rolling pasture land peppered with mature live oaks and towering pines.

But the most magnificent thing on the entire property was his impeccable herd of stocky quarter horses. They could often be found grazing beneath the shade of one of those massive oaks.

I hopped out of the truck and approached the group, asking if they had seen a bay or a black horse. The older man lifted his head to look at me, his eyes red-rimmed and his face looking like it had aged ten years in the two days behind him. He could barely find words and instead held up seven fingers. Seven vanished horses. A picture of his herd flashed through my mind. Seven more lives stolen by the current.

I wished the group of them good luck and got back into the truck.

"Are Jacky and Gray-Gray there?" Ruth asked from her car seat.

"No, honey. We're still looking," I replied, choking on my tears.

I pulled back onto our road and headed south again.

The man's pasture was on the left, and water poured from it and down the road. A few of his remaining cows stood in the middle of the street, and a plywood sign hung on a tree just beyond them, spray-painted with the words "COWS IN ROAD."

As I approached his home, I saw his tall wood staircase had been ripped from the porch and tossed into the forest on the far side of the property, along with a number of other unrecognizable items. Then something else came into focus: four hooves sticking straight up in the air from beneath the ditch. I shot my hand back and covered Ruth's eyes. One of his beautiful seven lay defeated, just feet from the road.

Tears poured out of my eyes. Tears for that sweet old man I never knew but had always respected. But tears of fear, too, that somewhere deep in the woods, my horses lay in the same sad state, reduced to nothing but soaking wet debris.

I struggled to focus. The water was still deep on both sides of the car, and I gripped the steering wheel, glancing at the purple life vest on the seat beside me.

Five miles and hundreds of flooded homes and vehicles later, I pulled into my best friend Mynde's driveway and breathed a sigh of relief at the sight of her.

Mynde was my first Louisiana friend. Downtown Boston to Baton Rouge had been no easy leap, and I was anything but graceful in the transition. I spoke the language of sarcasm and didn't believe college football held priority over the NFL. I had never eaten a crawfish and had never heard of a roux. I wondered if I would ever fit in.

Then Mynde came along. Through her, I began to believe there could be people for me here. People who would laugh at my jokes and enjoy my bland cooking. People who could see my heart and understand it was just packaged and delivered a little differently than their norm. Mynde thinks I'm funnier than I am, and she doesn't care that I still don't know how to peel a crawfish.

She met me on the porch with a hug, neither one of us sure what words could work. Ruth ran past me to find Mynde's two young boys, and I was grateful for her ability to be distracted.

Once inside, I collapsed on the couch. Moments later, Brad and Mynde's husband, Matt, returned from trying to rescue a friend's parents from a neighborhood a few miles away. They had launched a boat onto one of our town's two main roads and traveled past a National Guard high-water vehicle that had sunk in the ditch. Then they approached our gas station, which was underwater. Fuel spewed from its tanks and poured into the water surrounding it.

As Brad and Matt made their way through the neighborhood, they passed endless rows of full-sized trucks completely submerged. The only thing you could see were the different-colored roofs of the cabs, reflecting in the sun.

When they reached the home of the friend's parents, built high above the others in the back of the neighborhood, they found everyone inside, safe and sound. After passing them some bottled water, they turned back, relieved but exhausted.

Back on the hill, my thoughts were interrupted by the sound of the tractor shifting gears from deep in the woods below us. Farther out, past the oak trees and magnolias and on past the barn to a third hill, Brad and Matt now worked to bury my horses.

"This is all my fault," I said, rubbing my face with the palms of my hands. "I failed them."

Tessa leaned over, her face stern.

"No, ma'am," she said. "I was with you, Karen. I walked with you. When you texted me and told me you couldn't get them out, I could not believe your words. I thought you were kidding. It scared me to death. This"—she gestured widely—"this is insane."

Her eyes were wide with determination, and I knew that, like me, she had been living with her own reel of images, the constant replay of events that turned us on a dime. No one understood how things got so out of hand, and so quickly.

I rested my head on my chair, once again wishing there was a fight in me big enough to believe it was true that the beautiful animals being laid in the ground as we spoke were not being placed there on account of my bad decision-making.

I wasn't sure I would ever be able to convince myself of that.

The evening sun sparkled on the pond, and I stared down the road to the left. I have walked many roads in my life, but no single path has ever brought me more joy than the little dirt road that runs through the center of the property I now call home.

On a normal day, this hour would find me making the descent toward the barn. Ruth would be asleep for the night. Brad would sometimes join me, but other days I would venture off alone with the two dogs at my side, the sun making a colorful exit in the sky behind us. I would pass the pond and cross the creek and marvel at the trees before me, towering high above my head, soft wisps of Spanish moss blowing gently in the breeze.

Those had been the moments I allowed myself to slow down for the day, to shift gears and unwind as I scratched the velvet muzzles of the noses that nickered soft greetings upon my arrival, long whiskers tickling the palm of my hand as the horses nosed for treats.

My eyes burned as I relived the memory, staring down the road that now seemed so impassable, its path lined with fear and brokenness. It was all washed away.

I pictured the sad scene our little family had stumbled upon a few days before: the fence on its side and the holes where Jack had been stuck in the wire that lined it.

I winced at the irony. I had spent months researching fence construction before we built it. I made charts to compare materials. I found what I believed to be the most horse-safe option possible—the perfect height; the perfect span between posts; the perfect wire to keep out predators, the opening of which was deemed the perfect size for a horse.

I had followed the countless suggestions for twisted, not welded, wire so that, in an accident, no one would be lacerated by broken welds. I had added the top line of 2x6 boards to add support and promote visibility for the horses' eyes. We had constructed runs off both stalls leading to the pasture so they never had to be contained in the barn, at risk of being trapped in a fire or under a fallen tree.

I had gone to every length I had thought possible to build a fence and enclosure that would somehow be the ultimate means of protection for my two treasured pets, and now that fence lay leveled before me, gaping holes where Jack had been caught, complicating both of their rescues. The fruits of my worry, tattered and destroyed in a heap.

We had walked through the barn that day and surveyed the ground beneath our feet. The current had swept it out so that it looked like an East Coast beach at low tide. Dips and crevices dug into the clay, producing an intricate web of tributaries. It was hard to walk without tripping and falling.

I had reached for the side of one of the stalls, and the large board of its construction jiggled out from within my hand. The screws of each board had broken in half by the power of the surge.

Goose bumps covered my arms as I pictured Brad standing in that same space the night of the flood, his life protected by those boards as he haltered each of my horses, water inching closer to his shoulders with each new second. My eyes grew wide as I shook each unrestrained board, horrified at the idea of them springing free with him in there, two terrified twelve-hundred-pound creatures on each side of him.

Brad looked up and caught my eyes just then. I felt like I had just watched someone die.

"I know," he mouthed as he ruffled Ruth's hair, shaking his head in agreement.

I breathed out, processing that new image, another potential scene that could have played out and left us both dead or stranded in the dark floodwaters. I wouldn't have known how to help him. I wouldn't have been able to see in the dim light to find him or get him back up. I wouldn't have been able to get the boat going to get him medical attention. I wouldn't have known what to do. Those boards breaking any sooner would have ended both of us in one way or another.

From my spot in the yard with Tessa, I scanned the woods, my eyes moving from tree to tree and my mind traveling back three days, when I had finally found the courage to wander into those woods in search of the boys.

It was dark and dismal in there, once you got far enough inside. The ground squished beneath my boots like a wet sponge. Water still dripped from the large, emerald-green magnolia leaves that hung just over my head.

I tripped and stumbled over the many piles of my belongings strewn across the forest floor, but I didn't care. I left them all there. I was searching for the only two things I demanded the woods return to me.

I followed the path of bright-white jump standards, poles, hay bales, and buckets. They led me like crumbs to where Grady lay in a heap, tangled in a magnolia tree. He was breathtaking in life, and somehow his death did not take that from him. His jet-black coat still shone as bright as ever, even though his eyes no longer did.

I collapsed at his feet and sat on the soggy ground beside him, crumbling under the reality of the moment. I had failed him so miserably.

I forced my words to come out, though my body fought every syllable. I was determined to talk to him. I needed him to know how sorry I was—sorry to have promised to protect him and to get him out of that terrible situation and to have not been able to follow through on that promise. He had trusted me, and that trust had landed him here, lifeless.

Staring at him, I felt the hope drain out of me. There would be no happy ending. The optimistic vision I had carried of my two boys grazing somewhere across town was not a reality. Grady was the one who would have made it. Jack had all but given up in my arms.

I did not want to leave Grady there. I wanted to

stay with what remained of him and protect whatever that was, to claim him in some way that differentiated his body from all the debris that surrounded it. Even more, I wanted to cling to that last bit of closeness we could have in this lifetime.

I studied his ears and his glossy black mane. I closed my eyes and could picture twirling that same hair in my fingers while I rode him around our property. Or the way I tugged on it while waiting to go into the ring at a show. Or softly brushing it in the stillness of our evening visits.

"Grady, you are so loved," I whispered to him.

Then I stood up at the sound of another voice deep on the other side of the woods.

"Mama, Mama," Ruth was calling.

I wandered back out, defeated and heavy, to another body I had failed. Emptiness crept upon me with each new step.

I shook my head at the memory, wishing a headshake could remove the hollowness I felt.

I took a sip of wine and set the cup on the arm of my chair, balancing it with my right hand as my eyes surveyed the scene before me.

Brad's workshop had been completely submerged, and it sat about a hundred feet from us, in total disarray. The metal siding on the wall facing us had given in to the beating, and the roll-up door next to it had crumpled and caved in. The building was full of all of Brad's tools that he had painstakingly maintained for years. Now they lay in rusting heaps, boxes of supplies piled haphazardly on each other wherever the water had chosen to drop them. Scraps of wood were suspended in light fixtures. It was eight hundred square feet of soggy trash.

I looked beyond the shop to the wood line, which was littered with debris. The trees and undergrowth had been like a filter of sorts as the water poured through, leaving tires, wood, and gas tanks high in the branches above.

I looked to the left and scanned my garden, thinking back to the endless hours Ruth and I had spent working on it. She had delighted in planting everything we thought would either be delicious or beautiful, and she had carefully maintained it with her own tiny hands. I had hauled in load after load of mulch, filling the intricate maze of paths, and we had brought about twenty rocks back from the banks of the Rio Grande in Southern Colorado to outline its front border just one week before the flood.

I've always equated gardens to home. Growing up, my father and I had tended a large plot beside the modest blue ranch where I was raised. It was the most magical thing we did together. Our little yard grew blackberries in one corner, just before the woods, and strawberries were tucked back even further, down a long path through the pine trees and hemlocks. We picked our harvest side by side. My dad was my hero, the man who could grow food.

Then, in my twenties, living in Boston, I couldn't contain my excitement when my roommate and I found our first apartment with outdoor space—a tiny six-foot-by-twelve-foot balcony, but there was nothing tiny about it. I could grow something there. I lined it with colorful ceramic pots and filled them with soil and herbs, and there, even in the heart of a huge city, I would sit in the sun and dig into the dirt on Saturday mornings.

Dirt has always been good for my soul.

In every home after that, I increased my gardening spread—more land, more garden—but then, when we moved to this house, the one we joyfully deemed our "forever home," I approached my growing with a new tenacity. This garden would be an investment in our future, a symbol of our permanent place there. This sunny plot needed plants that grew roots, just as we would.

I planted perennials, fruit trees, berries, and herbs. I built its borders up with rocks, the most solid of foundations, permanent objects for our permanent home.

But now, from my spot at the top of the hill, all I could see was destruction. Our sweet garden was leveled—the mulch gone, the fruit trees bent at forty-five-degree angles, some plants dead and others ripped out completely. It had been uprooted, and so had I, my foundation unsettled.

I shook my head with frustration and stared up at the sky. The day was drawing to an end, and the colors high above us seemed so optimistic. Peach, purple, and orange blazed down on us like a grand finale to an amazing show. But there was nothing grand here. This show was terrible.

Ruth walked over to where we were sitting and put her hand on my arm.

"Where is my dad?" she asked, studying my face. She could hear the tractor below and saw Brad's and Matt's trucks in the driveway.

My eyes searched the woods as if looking for him, but really I was searching my heart for the right words and the right time to say those words. As each day had passed, my hope for finding the horses had worn thinner and thinner. Now, as the reality of their deaths became as real as the hole that had been dug in the ground for them, I knew she deserved honesty. She needed to know there was no point in continuing to look for them or to worry about their whereabouts as I knew she was.

I studied her face, so kind and so compassionate. Her gaze held such hope.

I couldn't yet bring myself to say the words I knew would change her outlook on life. I wasn't ready to deliver that blow.

"Daddy is with Uncle Matt in the woods, working on some stuff," I said, rubbing her back softly. "He'll be back in a bit."

Maybe I was delaying things for myself. Maybe it helped me to see her running and playing and laughing. Maybe I needed this small bit of normal for a little while longer.

Chapter 3

I STOOD IN THE middle of Brad's workshop a few mornings later, rubber gloves on my hands, scrubbing my way through a pile of rusted screwdrivers. The air was dank and musty, and the only thing keeping me from pulling a Dumpster up alongside the building and throwing everything out was my dad, who had driven across the country the day before and stood beside me now, sorting and restoring everything he could get his hands on.

It was the fifth day I'd spent salvaging flooded possessions, and I was about done with it.

Brad had retrieved my horse trailer from the woods as soon as the water had gone down, and I had tackled that first. I watched as he pulled the trailer up the hill behind the tractor on that first day. It had floated away and then been stopped by a mass of trees just past the barn. It had a long gash along its side, and all of its lights were broken. It dripped with dark brown sludge.

Sandy mud was stuck in the lock, and I struggled to open the door. When it finally swung open, I stood back and surveyed the little space full of my cherished things. The tiny closet in the front housed almost all of my stuff. I wasn't a girl with a closet full of clothes, and I wasn't into shoes. I didn't have a collection of jewelry, and electronics didn't make me flutter. My heart was in a tack room. I had spent my lifetime storing up leather and cotton and brass, every piece of which had a story.

I yanked first at a long black boot bag. My brother had given it to me for Christmas years before, and I could still see his narrow handwriting on the card. He wrote the best cards. I placed it gently on the ground at my feet and then reached for my saddle. I had bought it a few years before as one of the biggest splurges of my lifetime, a celebration for an exciting promotion at work. But the gesture was bigger than that on the day I purchased it, as it was the same day I was nursing the wound of yet another failed round of infertility treatments. Riding had been a helpful distraction.

I hung what remained of the saddle on my thigh and ran my index finger along its light brown seat. A glob of sludge came with it. I shook it off my hand, then propped the saddle against the back wheel of the trailer.

For hours, I stood there, reliving the stories of each muddy thing. Remembering where each item had gone with me and where it had come from. There wasn't much of it, and it wasn't the fanciest stuff available, but it was mine, and the stories that came with all of it were mine as well.

Somewhere in the process, I began to notice the similarities between me and those things. Dull and distorted. Hardly identifiable beneath the thick shell of mud encasing it all.

I picked up each item, knowing it had once been of value to me, but when I scraped the mud off, I found something that seemed incapable of being restored. Cracked leather. Warped and bloated wood. Moldy cotton, stained with faded colors. None of it would ever be as strong or as beautiful as it once was.

At one point I wanted to throw my hands up, toss every single thing in the trash, change my clothes, wash my hands, and just walk away. I didn't want to give up on those things I once loved or cherished, but I couldn't imagine any of them ever being brought back to their original luster. Besides, the road it would take to get them there seemed exhausting, the process too involved, the pile too big, the contents of those piles too far gone.

But somehow that parallel of connection between those things and me made me feel that giving up on those piles would be like giving up on myself. So I salvaged and I sprayed and I scrubbed and I cleaned every last thing I could. I was fighting for my soul as much as I was fighting for the objects in my hands.

I looked at the trailer now, standing at the top of the driveway. Brad and I had scrubbed it and cleaned it too, and then, when that hadn't felt like enough, we had sanded every scratch and gash and repainted it. Now Ruth was playing with my mom in front of it, and it looked brand new under the hot sun.

My parents had called the day after the flood and asked if they should come down to help. Generally I wasn't one to ask for help, but I had never wanted their presence or their support more than I did right then, and so they came. They packed up their car with things we needed and drove the twenty-four-hour haul from Boston to Baton Rouge without a second thought.

I watched Ruth as she played with her toys. We had found more of them in the woods, and I was grateful she was getting to play. More than that, I was grateful for the break my mother was giving her from me. I wanted to be better for Ruth. I wanted to cry less and be braver. But I hadn't figured out how to do that just yet.

I watched the two of them erupt in giggles as Ruth played with a faded pink water pistol, and I smiled.

Then I turned back to my task in the workshop and dumped a new pile of tools onto the bench with a groan. My dad, hunched over the workbench, scrubbed the rust from a drill with silent determination.

We had spent three days working within the confines of that hot metal shop. First we had emptied it, sorting through pile after pile of trash and yanking out endless sheets of soggy insulation. After that, we had scrubbed the walls with bleach and pressure washed the floor. Now we were working on cleaning and preserving the tools that had survived.

A few hours later, I set the wrench I had just cleaned into the tall red toolbox by my side.

My phone dinged with a text message. I peeled the latex gloves off my fingers, lifted my mask from my face, and slid my phone up and out of the back pocket of my sweat-soaked shorts.

As I scanned the words on my screen, I became infuriated. A friend who lived across the country thought the flood made perfect political fodder. It wasn't the first time in the days behind me that I'd felt confused by a person's lack of perspective. While our community linked arms and trudged through the aftermath in a unified fashion, some people had not joined in. They seemed content to stand on the sidelines—or, worse, to stand in the middle and break us all apart. I had no space inside me for those who weren't grief-stricken along with us and working to mend some of what was broken here.

I pushed my phone back in my pocket and looked over at my dad. He had on his tall green mud boots and stood in front of our window fan, swigging a bottle of water. He was drenched in sweat and looked a bit aged.

The world needed more people like my dad. Louisiana needed more people like my dad. *I* needed more people like my dad. We needed people who, even from the across the country, understood the need for people with a willingness to pull on their boots and get into this murky mess with us. People who were willing to get dirty for no reason other than to fix something or someone who was broken.

I couldn't deal with the people who opted to stay clean and tidy on the banks of it, judging things they couldn't see from far away.

I took a seat next to the shop and guzzled my water. The building was starting to look a lot like its pre-flood self, and it felt good. I stared down the dirt road toward the barn as my dad walked up.

"Let's head down there now," he said, wiping his gloves on his pants and twisting the cap off his water bottle.

"I'm good," I responded absently. I didn't want to go down there right then. I didn't know if I ever wanted to go back down there. What I wanted to do was create small pockets of normalcy for myself where I didn't have to face the reality of any one thing head-on. The barn was too far gone. Nothing would ever be normal there again. That structure and everything that surrounded it was a big, glaring symbol of everything that was wrong.

My dad looked at me, his expression hovering somewhere between empathy and frustration. He wanted more fight from me. He had a unique ability to make me want to do better than I thought I could.

He had raised me to ask more of myself. That had helped me as a kid. I was determined back then, always brushing myself off after a bad collision in soccer or getting back on a horse that had dumped me in the dirt. I wasn't easily deterred.

This was different. This wasn't a skinned knee or a busted elbow. *I* was the thing that was busted. More so with each passing day.

"Let's get some stuff out of the woods, and that will be a start," he said, turning toward our ATV that was parked by the shop. He climbed onto it, patting the passenger seat next to him.

An hour later, we stood staring into the barn. Mounds of my muddy stuff were now piled under its roof. We'd found more of it in the woods than I expected—yard tools, wheelbarrows, chairs, tables, and even a few dilapidated hoses.

I didn't know how I felt about any of it. I had been motivated to fix Brad's workshop. That building and everything in it still had a purpose. But I didn't understand the point in clinging to anything about *this* building and *this* stuff. It felt like the first step in a process I wasn't sure I would be able to finish. One more inevitable failure I wasn't up for recognizing. Maybe it would be easier to walk away from all of it. To find a new hobby—one that didn't involve living things.

We headed back up to the house, and I found my mother inside with Ruth, getting ready for dinner.

Ruth sat in the middle of the living room, coloring in one of her many horse-themed books. She had chosen a picture of a herd of horses standing in a creek, drinking water. She had a red crayon and was coating the water and the horse in the bold hue with fast strokes. Occasionally she would look up and stare outside in silence.

I followed her gaze, past the pond and down the road toward the barn.

"You need to talk to her about this," my mom whispered. "She's been asking about them all day."

I nodded, knowing I needed to do it but still not sure which words would be best. Too much time had passed, and now, instead of buffering her from the pain, I was suspending her in this state of not knowing. I knew she needed closure, not more confusion.

I left the kitchen and found a box in my closet that held beautiful model horses I had purchased for her last birthday—before learning that two-year-olds have no business owning model horses. One of them was a big bay racehorse, just like Jack. I lifted it gently from the box and carried it back to the living room.

I sat down on the soft rug next to Ruth and rubbed her back.

"Hi, Mom," she said, without looking up from her coloring.

I paused for a second, wondering if there was any way around this, any way to get through this without having to crush her in the way I knew it would. The words on the tip of my tongue would change things for her. They would change *her*.

I took a deep breath and rolled a lock of her light blonde hair between my fingers.

"Ruthie," I began. "I know you have been looking very hard for Jacky and Gray-Gray these past few days. We all have been. We all had hoped they were able to swim out of the water. But they couldn't, baby. They aren't going to be coming back home."

"Why?" she asked, coloring with renewed fervor, refusing to look up at me.

We had just gone through the death talk when our dog Hunter passed away last year. She still asked for Hunter and, in all honesty, she still, to that day, was mad at God for taking her dog. I didn't want to implicate God in another loss, but I did want to be honest about the reality of death.

"Baby, when the flood happened," I began, "the water went up and up and got higher and higher. It was so high and so fast that it got hard for Jacky and Grady to swim. And when they couldn't swim in it anymore, God took them out of the water and brought them to be with Him, where they would be so safe and not hurt."

The muscles in her face tightened as she processed my response. I had never before seen the expression on her little face in that moment. I didn't recognize her demeanor. She was mad.

"I have this horsey for you," I continued, offering the model horse. "He's going to be your friend and keep you company when you miss Jacky and Grady, okay?"

She took the horse from me, set it down on the rug beside me, and got up and walked out of the room.

Chapter 4

A NEW WEEK DAWNED. I listened to Brad get ready for work in the other room as I sat on the couch, staring out the massive window at the water line on the roof of our workshop. Water lines were fitting, I supposed. I knew the building was more or less repaired, but the water line remained there like a scar, a permanent reminder of the damage the floodwaters had done, just like the raised line that marked where stitches once patched a wound back together.

The water goes down, the building gets gutted and repaired, and everything goes back to normal. Casual observers may not even be able to tell it had flooded, if it weren't for that water line. No, water lines insist on staying. They mark their victims, refusing to let them forget what happened to them once upon a time.

I knew normal was trying to creep back in on me. My parents had returned to Boston, the water had returned to the river, and Brad was returning to work. Every sound he made in the other room was normal, even—audible indicators of each step of our old routine. I heard him turn on the water as he shaved. I heard the sound of the shower door slam as he entered and left it. I heard metal hangers scrape the bar in his closet as he searched for something to wear. I heard the buzz of his toothbrush, his final step.

Before I knew it, he stood before me, ready for work, looking far too normal in the sea of chaos that surrounded us. He walked over to where I sat and bent down to kiss my forehead. Then he looked me square in the eyes and said, "Find something to do today, baby. Get out of this house and go somewhere."

I saw the pain he felt for me in his eyes and wished I could pull myself together, maybe find some courage in this whole thing, if only to send him off into the world for the day not worrying about me.

But I couldn't do it. My eyes told my story. I would stay home.

A moment later, I heard the door shut behind him and the sound of his footsteps descending the porch stairs. Tears welled up in my eyes and poured out. I let them come, freely saving my fight for later on in the morning, when Ruth would wake up and I would have to be brave.

I took a sip of my coffee and stared at my mug, the same mug I filled with coffee each day. It was a souvenir from a tiny restaurant called Plane View, which is housed inside of an equally tiny airport on the little island where my grandmother was raised. My grandfather loved to take us there in the summer to eat lunch and watch the planes come and go. His eyes would light up as he watched each shiny machine take flight.

My grandfather had been remarkable. There was no end to the number of things he pursued in his long and colorful life. He was an engineer, holding degrees in both math and physics. He was a fireman, a photographer, a piano player, and a composer of upbeat love songs. In his younger years, he played softball, hockey, and the trombone. He ran for the school board, got involved in local politics, and was an outspoken supporter of the Red Cross. He tinkered with model trains, could rewire a house, and sang bass in our church choir. He was endlessly devoted to the work of God, often hosting missionaries in his home, cooking for Bible studies, and driving the van every summer for Vacation Bible School.

As a young man, he bridged the gap between the homebound and our church by developing a radio room behind the sanctuary so he could broadcast and tape the sermons. That way, no one had to miss out on the weekly service. He would often joke it was just as much a ministry to him, as making the tapes required playing back the sermon five times. He said that was how long it took for the message to penetrate his admittedly hard head.

My grandfather had the kind of wit that can only come from being razor sharp and a genuinely good-hearted human being. His eyes danced, and he could laugh without making a sound. He set the bar for how I wanted to live my life. He lived his own so completely.

Still, I never understood his love for airplanes. It

didn't make sense, knowing he had nearly died in a plane sixty years before.

I placed the mug on the table and stared at the red and blue cartoon plane painted on the side of it. Its colors were fading a bit after six years of daily washing. On the day I had bought it at Plane View, Grandy, as we called him, stood in line with me as I waited to pay and chuckled when he saw its silly logo. Why on earth was a penguin flying the plane?

I told him I would use it every day and think of him. He looked down at me with a grin. He knew I didn't need a mug to think about him. We were buddies—grand companions—and he knew he was always on my mind, even when we were apart. I think we both knew, in some way, that he was fading from me on that July afternoon, but I don't think either of us knew how fast or that it would be the last day we'd view planes together.

In a short blink from that sunny day, I found myself standing in a pew at our church, forced to say goodbye to Grandy far sooner than I felt was fair. I stared at the choir loft, willing his figure to return to his now vacant spot. I could almost hear his sweet voice belting out each word of his favorite hymn:

> When we walk with the Lord in the light of
> His Word,
> What a glory He sheds on our way!
> While we do His good will, He abides with
> us still,
> And with all who will trust and obey.

Not a shadow can rise, not a cloud in the
skies,
But His smile quickly drives it away;
Not a doubt or a fear, not a sigh or a tear,
Can abide while we trust and obey.

Not a burden we bear, not a sorrow we share,
But our toil He doth richly repay;
Not a grief or a loss, not a frown or a cross,
But is blessed if we trust and obey.

Trust and obey, for there's no other way
To be happy in Jesus, but to trust and obey.

—John H. Sammis

As the song finished, I couldn't help but feel his love for that song was just as confusing as his love for planes. I studied the words with grief-stricken skepticism. Not a shadow can rise? Not a cloud in the skies? No fear? No tears?

The lyrics were poetic and beautiful, but my grandfather had seen a few clouds during his darkest days. Shadows did rise on him. Fear, and maybe even some tears, had to have been present when he was shot out of that plane in World War II.

It was his twenty-third bombing mission, and it should have been his last, but instead of going home, he was captured by enemy troops and imprisoned at the foot of the Alps. He was tortured and interrogated so much that it took fifty years for him to speak a word of it.

I closed the hymnal and placed it in the rack

before me, wondering if I had inherited his courage. I was a watered-down version of him, not quite as intelligent or witty, and certainly nowhere near as dazzling. If I was faced with suffering in my lifetime, would I be able to follow his lead in such a way that I would sing God's praises afterward? Or would I yell at Him for failing me?

I wondered what happened between that prison camp in Austria and the day he decided "Trust and Obey" was a hymn he could relate to. A hymn containing a message he would live by. A hymn with words he could deem precious.

I traced the outline of the logo on the mug with my thumb as the memory of that day played through my mind. I wanted to talk to him so badly. He could have told me how to get out of this. He would have known what to do. He had gotten through much worse and even managed to reclaim his sparkle.

I set the mug down and got up to open the drawer where I kept some of my treasures connected to him: an old compass, a black-and-white picture of him, his camera, a toy train—and his memoirs. I pulled the stack of papers out of the drawer and sat them next to my mug in front of me. I wanted to feel close to him for a moment, and his words on paper were as good as I could get.

I began to read the story of his life during the war. He had been thirty thousand feet in the air when his massive flying fortress was shot straight through and began falling from the sky. He stayed on board while the plane burned as it fell so he could destroy all the radar equipment, ensuring it was kept from the Germans. When he finally jumped out of that doomed plane, he counted the number of seconds until it was safe to open his chute.

He landed in a foreign country in the middle of a raging war and surrendered to enemy troops. He was twenty-one years old.

I put the pages down and took a sip of my coffee, staring over my mug to survey our backyard. I studied the wood line that runs the length of our property, each bent and broken tree a reminder of the battle—the one I could not win. I saw the endless piles of brush and limbs lying in debris-covered heaps on their sides, defeated, and remembered everything else that wasn't spared by the water's swift current.

I stared at my hands in disbelief. They had been torn and blistered from the grip that wasn't strong enough to overpower the water. I pictured my sweet horses being ripped from them and wondered how any of it could be true. Why hadn't my arms been stronger? Why hadn't God tamed the storm, if only for a minute? I hung my head, reliving those last few moments with my boys. I remembered how soft Jack's coat had felt as I rubbed his jaw and tried to comfort him.

Today, my body and mind still felt anchored with fright. My limbs seemed afraid to move, terrified I would suddenly be within death's reaches once more. It made no difference that I had stepped off our boat onto firm ground, walked into my home, and dried off. I could still feel it. I still felt soaked by the rain. I still felt the tension of anticipation each time the boat slammed into the trees. I still felt as if that night might engulf me. Whenever I closed my eyes in search of sleep, I found myself watching as we almost flipped. Understanding what would have come next. Wondering how my daughter would have gotten by without her parents.

Death came so close that I could see it, like a deleted scene on the cutting-room floor. The water may have receded from our yard, but it continued to close in on my soul, threatening to drown me, even on each bright and sunny day that had followed since.

Then, out of the corner of my eye, I saw the little penguin pilot smiling back at me, and I was brought back to my grandfather. I could almost see him floating through the sky, watching the burning planes and his comrades falling on all sides of him. Lives ended before his eyes. Massive machines lay in heaps of rubble on the ground below. He no doubt wondered what his future held once his feet hit that foreign soil.

He noted in his memoirs that he still loved the sky. I wondered if I could ever love the woods again.

I thought about Brad's suggestion and knew leaving home meant driving down the streets of my tattered town and seeing each home that had been leveled. My heart was broken at the thought of each family whose life's work and memories were covered in crusty mud and set out in heaps by the road. Leaving home meant coming face-to-face with the wound our community had sustained, a wound I wasn't sure could be healed.

How could we repair and restore everything that had been destroyed? Hope seemed like a distant dream that had been swallowed up by the floodwaters too. Had we been forgotten?

I imagined my grandfather felt the same way after his capture. He sat alone, in solitary confinement, with no lights and no food, being interrogated. He noted remembering his good times and wondering if he would ever return to them or make any more memories. Then, when things already seemed to be too much and he had surely had enough, he marched one hundred eighty miles to freedom. He was just skin and bones. Dirty and ragged clothes hung off what remained of his once regal frame. He was exhausted and unrecognizable but determined to power through and find his way home to his future.

I needed his story this morning. I needed him to paint that picture, the picture of his darkest days, for me. I had to understand what he had come back from.

I stared at the black-and-white photo of him and remembered the man he became. He lit up my world with his eyes. He was hilarious, courageous, and genuine. More importantly, he was endlessly devoted to God, a living witness to the hope that comes from a life spent following Jesus Christ. Things did get nasty for him, but he trusted, and he obeyed, and he was delivered from it.

I studied his face in the photo. Every muscle in his body laughed. I noticed his Bible open before him in the shot and managed a small smile. He was "walking in the light of His Word," as the hymn said. It was what he did. As a young newlywed, he and some friends had started a Bible study group called the Saturday Morning Saints. They would meet every week and study Scripture over pancakes and coffee. He didn't stop going until he died, sixty years later.

The picture was taken at a meeting of the Saturday Morning Saints. I knew the exact spot where he sat. I had climbed up and down the stairs in that background more times than I could count. I had sat on those grainy steps and shared snacks with my cousin, Kim, year after year. *Surely*, I thought, *if I could just go back to those stairs and back to the comfort of that building and that community, then things would feel better for me.*

I closed my eyes and pictured the church, standing tall in the center of our little town. I could almost smell the boxwoods that lined the sidewalk leading to its huge red doors, their soft scent beckoning me on a warm summer day. I could still see the crisp white sanctuary, the crimson cushions lining each familiar row, the pale blue hymnals full of songs I knew by heart. I could see my grandparents and my mother standing in the choir loft, sweetly singing each word of the song "What a Friend We Have in Jesus" in matching black robes with red sashes.

I knew every nook of that building as if it was my own house. I knew where they hid the crackers, the crayons, and the construction paper. I could run through the basement with my eyes closed and not hit a single wall or doorway. I had the library memorized and would sit, entranced, as I flipped through each page of the stories that lined the bottom shelf in the children's section. I would lie on the soft gray carpet in the foyer, not knowing any difference between that spot and my own living room floor. I could picture all of the familiar faces that greeted me around each corner. Each one knew me well. Each one prayed for me with every inch I grew. Each one felt more like family than friend.

As I sat in my living room in Louisiana, a world away, I realized for the first time in years how far I was from the comfort of that home. I hadn't even realized how comforting it had been until that very moment. But even if I turned around and ran back as fast as I could, very little of that home would still be where I had left it. Most of those familiar faces were gone. My prayer warriors had finished their fights. Even the building had been renovated, a sidewalk now running where the boxwoods once stood.

I closed my eyes, tears burning behind their lids, demanding to surface. When I opened them, I looked at my grandfather's Bible in the photograph, open on the table in front of him. I studied his laughing face. I could nearly hear that laughter.

All I could think of in that moment were the sweet words of Zechariah 1:3: "Return to me, and I will return to you." I loved those words. They were so simple.

Unfortunately, the process was not. I wanted to return. I wanted to go back. I wanted to plant myself on one of those soft red cushions and feel the security they offered me. But I couldn't. I had created this solitude. I had left. I had wandered far from home, and now there was no home to return to anymore.

Chapter 5

"I MISS MY JACKY," Ruth said, rubbing her eyes as I put her down in her bed.

"I know, baby. I miss him, too," I said. "I miss them both so much."

I pushed the hair from her eyes and kissed her forehead, then pulled her plush blanket up to her chin. I wished a kiss could fix everything for her.

"I want to show you something," I said, getting up from her bed and shutting off the lights. I had snuck in earlier and stuck an array of glow-in-the-dark stars on her ceiling. Two extra-large ones were affixed right above her head.

"Jacky and Grady are both up in heaven with Jesus," I said. "They are so safe now, and they don't have to be scared. But they miss you, too, so much. Whenever you miss them, look up at your sky and picture them way up there, loving you from heaven, okay?"

"I like that," she said, snuggling her head into her pillow.

We said her prayers together, thanking God for Jacky and Grady and asking Him to be extra sweet to them while they got used to their new home. Then we reminded Him that they both like carrots—a lot.

I pulled her bedroom door closed and stopped in the hallway, surveying the large, wooden, framed artwork of Jeremiah 29:11 that hung from the wall. "For I know the plans I have for you, declares the Lord," it said. "Plans to prosper you and not to harm you. Plans to give you hope and a future."

I read its words again and again, wondering if doing so would help make sense of it.

The truth is, I wasn't sure I loved those words anymore. I didn't know if I could trust them. I wanted to follow my grandfather's lead. I wanted to respond to the tug in my heart to go to God with this. But I didn't know if I could. God was confusing me.

I thought back to the day when I had brought that sign home and hung it on the wall. It was a few months after Ruth had been born, and I wanted that verse to have a permanent place in our home, reminding me of the four years I had waited for her birth and the comfort I had found in those words during that time. But looking at it now, I didn't see hope there. All I saw was a broken promise.

"These are Your plans?" I whispered softly, studying the soft, white, cursive lines that covered the light brown wood.

I rarely confronted God out loud. Even at a whisper, my words felt unruly. But I was so hurt. I felt so abandoned. Wronged. Confused.

I pictured Ruth on the other side of that wall, snuggling a purple unicorn with all of her might as she prayed for her dead pets, and it made me so angry. Why was my two-year-old going through this?

My tears came back as I pictured the horses thrashing in the water and then my neighbors dragging the contents of their destroyed homes to the curb—homes that held their history and, they had thought, their future.

God could have stopped it.

I stared at those words on my wall, watching as the hope seeped out of them, confusion filling the void they left.

I turned and headed down the hall toward the kitchen, not knowing what to do with the emotions boiling up from within me. Brad had gone to his friend's house for the evening to help hang sheetrock in his flooded house, so I had the last few hours of daylight to spend alone with my thoughts. But I didn't want my thoughts or my newfound solitude. I wanted my pets. I wanted my normal.

I missed my evening walks to visit the horses after Ruth went to bed. I missed my peaceful time with them, watching the sun set on the hill while they munched on their hay. On some days I would grab a few brushes and work the dirt of the day out of their shiny coats. But more often than not, I would just lay my head against Jack's tall withers and scratch him gently while I watched the orange sky sparkle through the intricate detail of the Spanish moss on the trees. Jack was happy to hold my weight with his frame in exchange for the attention.

I felt so lost. The world was upside down on all sides, and the few hours of sunlight that remained seemed to cast its rays on the reality of it all, like a magnifying glass on my soul.

I had no direction anymore. I had no light of my own. Everything was dark.

I was tired of the noise from the day, and I was sick of the news. I was exhausted with the status updates. I was angry at the world and the people in my life who had moved on with ease while I was stuck here in mourning and chaos. I needed to create some distance for myself. I needed some silence.

Walking into the kitchen, I stared out the window at my garden. It was still covered in trash. The leaves of my once beautiful plants were now withered and brown. A tiny young apple tree had nearly fallen on its side.

I hadn't been out to tend to the garden yet. Far more pressing things had needed to be handled first, like flooded buildings and buried pets. But my soul found comfort in that garden. It was where I went to work out my thoughts. Something about digging into dirt grounded me. I needed that right about then.

I slid my feet into my flip-flops and walked outside, a dog on each side of me. But as I stepped into the garden, I immediately felt frustration. The mess was out of control. It would take forever to get it back to its old self.

Still, I knew I had to start somewhere. I began

working my way through the tattered plot, collecting trash, yanking out dead plants, and cutting broken branches that hung, tangled, from tired trees.

As I hunched over, unearthing a weed from below a toppled terra-cotta pot, my mind wandered to that verse on our wall. I didn't know what to make of those words anymore. Everything about this experience felt like harm.

It had been two weeks since the flood, and countless people had tried to infer what God's will had been through it. It seemed like every person had a different opinion of how heavy His hand had been in it. Was He punishing us? I didn't think so. Was He hands off and ambivalent to the struggles of our little town? No, I didn't think that, either.

I would sit in silence and listen to the discussions and want to get up and walk away. But I knew walking away wouldn't save me from this one. Wherever I walked, the same questions swirled in my head. It all boiled down to one big question: "Why this?"

I knew God loved me. I knew I probably frustrated Him to no end at times, but I also knew His love didn't depend on my having good decision-making skills. I have always felt well known by God. I've always felt understood by Him, so much so that a part of my identity, even as I'd wandered all these years, hinged on my being known by Him.

I just could not figure out how a God who knew me so well could let one of my worst fears materialize into a horror movie before my eyes. He knew how much I loved my horses. He knew I was a worrier. He knew I couldn't handle news stories, even, where animals were hurt. He knew I hadn't seen the movie *Hancock* because, ten years ago, someone had told me the dog in the movie got hurt.

Given all that, I didn't feel I had been protected by a loving God who had good plans for me. I was confused by the fact that, knowing me, He chose not to put His foot down on this one. Why didn't He put the brakes on this in some way, saying, "No, she cannot handle that; it would be too much"?

I dug a little deeper and yanked one final root out of the ground, then tossed the wilted bush in my compost pile.

I thought back to those four years we spent waiting for Ruth. The endless trips to the doctor. How we worked our way down a list of arbitrary diagnoses.

First they had ruled out the big stuff, the easy stuff, like if I had a working uterus. Then we moved into the "medical mystery" part, the part where nothing can really be identified in medical terms. The place where even when something is identified, it's accompanied by a percentage that changes with age and a long list of other factors, none of which make sense to someone without a degree in reproductive endocrinology. They can anchor what's happening with a few absolutes, but the rest of it is fluid. It's all in constant motion and surrounded by question marks rather than facts. Very little of it can be seen or quantified.

I could still see the top of my chart, *unexplained infertility* written in all caps at the top. It was infuriating. I wanted a specific term. At the very least, after the three years of tests and procedures, I would have liked a diagnosis that didn't include the word *unexplained*. But none of that was possible. There was no word. The answers were hidden somewhere in my complex anatomy and could not be fully explained or understood, even by the best doctors who had years of education and research on their side.

I walked over to the little apple tree and drove a stake into the ground a few feet from its base. I tied its tiny trunk to the stake and tightened it and wondered if this flood had caused God to feel as "unexplainable" to me as my infertility had.

I had the basics. I believed in Him, and I knew He was inherently good, not vengeful or destructive to His people. But then what? How had He allowed me to get here? It seemed like such a harsh reality. Why no miracle? Why no parted sea? What was the criteria God used to deem someone worth saving from ruin? Why were so many of us overlooked? Why 146,000 flooded homes? Why the cancer? Why the sick children? Why the neglect? Why any of it?

If He had the power, which I believed He did, then why did He not intervene to save His children? Why the suffering?

My thoughts sounded exactly like they had all

those years ago, after each failed round of treatments. I would read the news and see horrifying stories of child abuse and neglect and think, *Why them and not me, Lord?* Why did criminals get babies to hurt, and I couldn't have one to love?

I didn't think God caused my infertility. I didn't think He was withholding a child from me. None of that was in line with how I knew God. I just didn't know why He wouldn't fix it when I knew He could. Why wouldn't He flip the switch on my "unexplainable" anatomy and give me the baby I prayed to receive? Where was the difficulty in all of that? At the very least, He could shut down the heinous people being let into the baby-making department. Level the playing field a bit.

I never pinned down the answer to all that back then, nor had I pinned down how I understood God in relation to it. I just used that verse from Jeremiah to visualize God planning a future for me that involved a baby *at some point*. I imagined a timeline only He could see. It was a mystery, but undoubtedly one with a happy ending, and I was okay with that. But the part where my heart wasn't filled with faith in God's plans for me as much as it was filled with determination to convince God of what His plans *should* be for me? That part was no good.

Then Ruth was born, and I believed her to be an answer to prayer and moved away from trying to sort out my beliefs on God's will. I had a new appreciation for those words from Jeremiah and the future promised there.

But in my present state of anger and confusion, I knew following that same path wasn't going to do the trick. This was not about waiting. This was entirely different. I was broken. I didn't understand God, and I wasn't convinced He hadn't abandoned me at a crucial point in my life.

I needed to know more about what happened when God first made that promise in the book of Jeremiah. I needed to take it from the walls of my house and from the pages of my Bible and make it come to life. Maybe then I would find rest from the voice in my head that was trying to convince me God didn't care about me anymore, that I had let Him down too many times to be His priority.

I picked up my tools and headed back into the house.

I sat down on the couch and opened my Bible to the book of Jeremiah. I hadn't read it in years. I'd just taken what I wanted from it and shut the book.

As I read, I saw the Jews in Babylon, driven from their city and brought into exile. I'm no scholar of the Bible, but I pictured them exhausted and running low on hope. They had been doing their own thing, ignoring God and worshipping the wrong stuff, and now they were in a bind. God had begged them countless times to cut it out, but they hadn't listened.

It all sounded pretty familiar. It sounded a bit like me.

Then, after all those years they spent denying God, and despite the fact that He was mad and discouraged by their abandonment of Him, He came to them through Jeremiah and made a promise. He promised that although things were bleak, He still had plans for them when they came back home. He said there would be an end to their suffering and that the future, though hard to see, was bright.

I read through the eleventh verse of the twenty-ninth chapter, where He makes that promise that was hanging on my wall, and smiled at the words on the page, highlighted in yellow. It was a promise to wanderers, a promise of hope in the midst of destruction. It was a call to keep seeking God even when your world is in ruins.

Then I read the next two verses and began to cry. Hidden right behind the place where I'd gone for comfort all those years was a new promise—a promise I had missed and that tugged at my soul. I grabbed a pink highlighter and ran it carefully across each word:

> "Then you will call on me and come and pray to me, and I will listen to you. You will seek me and find me when you seek me with all your heart."
>
> —Jeremiah 29:12–13, niv

Somewhere in my heart, I knew I had not ever done that before. I'd never expended much effort into seeking. I knew the song "Seek Ye First," but that was about where it stopped. I wasn't even sure how to go about doing it. I just knew I was ready to try.

The next morning, the smell of freshly brewed coffee filled the air as I stood in my kitchen, filling my mug and biting into a slightly overripe banana. I didn't have any real direction for the day—I never did anymore—so I had my phone in my hand, ready to scour social media to let the flood-related needs of the day dictate my direction. Things were changing rapidly, as people were leaving shelters and heading home to assess the status of what was left behind. Our food bank had been destroyed, families had no clothes, and cleaning supplies were in high demand. No doubt, with a little looking, I would find something that needed to be done.

I logged on and noticed I had new notifications. I clicked the icon and scanned down to where it said I had "memories for the day."

My heart dropped when I saw the picture. It was Ruth with Jack, taken on that same day one year earlier. She was a year old and stood brushing him with the confidence of a teenager. Jack could do that for you. Make you feel safer and more confident than you should have felt in the presence of an animal as large as he was. It was his nature. He was a gentle giant.

Thoroughbreds like Jack, former racehorses particularly, are often high strung and perpetually wired. Some horses bred like Jack come off the track and never calm down. But my sweet Jack came off that racetrack and instantly relaxed into his new role as "backyard pet who rarely gets ridden." It was as if he had been waiting his whole life to be loved and brushed by a little girl—and my little girl was his girl.

I stared down at that once sweet picture, the hollow pit of grief that now lived in me growing bigger. I remembered the day in living color. It was a beautiful one. A laid-back Saturday, the kind where you're more concerned with being together as a family than with chasing a project. Just three people enjoying their life with their pets for a few hours.

I wondered if I could ever love that picture or the memory of that day—or any other day—again.

I opened the camera roll on my phone and started flipping through each picture, daring my emotions to come out like I was opening a closet door in a house of horrors, but I was determined to take an inventory of all that had been stolen from me on that stormy day. I wanted to lay all of my losses out on the table along with everything else I had already accounted for.

I found the picture of Ruth as a newborn, bundled in her stroller and locking eyes with Jack in a way that seemed they had known each other for years. Then the one from the afternoon when she insisted on setting up her little blue pool in front of Grady's stall so they could play together in the June heat. Grady was often hard-headed and a little bit of a bully to full-grown humans, but he had the softest spot in him for little ones. He might walk all over an adult, but he tiptoed around my little girl.

There were pictures from when I set a Pack 'n Play in front of Jack's stall so he could entertain Ruth while I worked in the barn. Shots of her in a walker, making countless rounds up and down the center aisle of the barn, much to everyone's amusement. Images of her sitting high up on Grady's back, the pride shining through her eyes. Moments captured during my first horse show after Ruth's birth, my smile conveying the joy I felt being back in the ring.

So many pictures documented in beautiful color and perfect light all of the silliness and delight that had been my daughter's nearly three years of life growing up alongside these two sweet and willing creatures—and now those pictures may as well have drowned too. They belonged in the woods, scattered with everything else, soggy with faded colors.

I stopped scrolling when I came to one with Hunter and Grady, both of them leaning toward Ruth in delight as she giggled at them from her green walker. *Those were the days*, I thought.

I studied Hunter. The contrast between my memory of him and of Grady felt so stark. Losing him had been difficult. I had picked him up as a puppy the week before my high school graduation. My mom had nearly lost her mind. I was too irresponsible for a puppy—I could barely take care of myself, let alone another living creature.

She and I look back on it now and laugh. Neither of us could have predicted the impact that tiny ball of fur would make on my life. He was able to do what my parents had only dreamed of doing. He convinced me to grow up.

We moved together to Boston, where I attended college, and I always managed to find apartments that would allow him to stay and roommates who loved his company almost as much as I did. Every year we spent together, I became a little less rebellious and a little more responsible.

We went everywhere together, and I became accustomed to having him by my side, a big ball of black and tan fluff who bounded along beside me through every major turn of my young adult life. When I met Brad and we decided to move to Louisiana, Hunter came along for the twenty-four-hour drive and rejoiced in the fenced-in yard waiting for him when we arrived in sunny Baton Rouge. By his city-dog standards, it was like having his very own dog park. Between our wedding, vacations, and holidays, I lost count of how many trips to and from Boston he made. We always preferred to be together, even if that meant two days in a car rather than three hours on a plane.

When we moved from our first house by the campus of Louisiana State University to a home with a barn and three acres, I thought he was going to explode with dog happiness. Sometimes I would go outside to work in the pastures and he would wander out there with me and lie down next to the horses in the shade.

He was growing up too, his rambunctious nature fading a little more every year. At one point, he turned the corner to where he was happier sitting and relaxing than running around at breakneck speed—and I could relate. The farm life fit both of us better than anything had before. I loved transitioning with him from city life to suburban life to our ultimate calling in the country. We had both found our niche in the world, and we had found it together.

Hunter was thirteen when Ruth was born, and he took to her the moment she arrived home. Sleeping was his preferred pastime at that age, but when Ruth was in her little swing, he would sit up, alert, and guard her as if he was bred for such a thing. He never missed a story time, loved when she began eating solid foods, and found the speed at which she moved to be quite accommodating, considering his lack of mobility. When she got older and could walk, they would hang out in the barn together. She would blow bubbles and babble at him with her little bald head planted in his fluff. He was happy just to be with her—and glad she couldn't run or jump yet.

I had been seventeen when I brought Hunter home,

and I was one month shy of thirty-three when he slipped away from me. He had been present for every major event in my life—a lifelong companion—and what a life it was.

I remember being mad at myself the first day I didn't cry after he had passed away. I had been anticipating his death for a while and doubted I would ever move on from it. But after a few days of guilt and confusion, I gave myself a break when I realized I was able to cope with losing him so well because of how complete his life had been and the peaceful nature of his passing. I was comforted by those two things.

His was the perfect life. I could not have asked for more when I picked him up on the coast of New Hampshire that sunny May morning. He was never hurt, never lost, never mistreated, and never sick, and when he was tired, he simply bowed out. He enriched every second of my life and made me a far better person than I could have been without him. There was nothing more I could expect. An ending like that allowed my soul to move on with a perfect memory and my appreciation of him intact.

I studied the picture and shook my head. That wasn't the case with Grady or Jack. None of what had comforted me through the loss of Hunter applied to Jack's and Grady's deaths. Their deaths were too tragic. Too brutal. Too confusing. I couldn't get to a place where I could grieve them peacefully. There was nothing peaceful about it. Pictures of them didn't bring fondness or sweet memories. They just brought me back to the boat, to watching them struggle through their horrible and uncalled-for deaths.

I set my phone down and wondered if this new grief-stricken version of me was permanent. Could sorrow become a personality trait, rather than a passing phase? Besides being messy and disorganized, was I now also perpetually sad? That's a pretty hard combo to sell at a dinner party.

I was stumped. I was in a deeper and darker spot than I had ever experienced before, and I had no idea how to set myself free from it.

I looked at Ruth, who was finishing up her last bite of cereal. We had to get out of the house. I looked out the window at the garden, brown and lifeless. It looked a lot like I felt. Maybe some new growth was in order.

"Where are we going?" Ruth asked as I buckled her into the car fifteen minutes later.

"The gardening store," I replied.

She nodded her head with a smile of approval, and we headed down the road.

I was grateful to find our favorite little nursery open. Nearly every structure on that street had been damaged or destroyed. This store had flooded too, but the owners had bounced back, given that they operated out of a relatively small metal building. A large sign with red letters was propped by the road:

"WE HAVE CLEANING SUPPLIES." I looked at it and wondered, "DO YOU HAVE PLANTS?"

I really didn't care what kind of plants they had. I just needed *a* plant. Something—anything—with roots and some color.

We walked along the outdoor aisles and grabbed the herbs and flowers that remained. There wasn't much, seeing as how it was the middle of August and we had just had a catastrophic weather event. But it was enough.

I filled a red wagon that looked like it had seen better days and pulled it through the doors to the cash register. A woman in front of me was checking out with a few bottles of bleach and a scrub brush. Her clothes and her hair were dirty and disheveled. Her face was sunken with exhaustion.

Suddenly I felt wrong somehow, standing behind her with my plants and my clean clothes. Was I flaunting my non-flooded home? I shifted uneasily, wondering if my priorities were off. Should I drop what I was doing and offer to follow her to her house and help gut it? I had, admittedly, been sidetracked by the pictures on my phone. I'd forgotten my ultimate goal for the day had been to help someone else. Instead, here I stood, dealing with my own self.

As the woman shuffled out the door, I couldn't help but consider how the flood had damaged us all. We were all, to varying degrees, cracked and warped versions of our pre-flood selves, exhausted from the never-ending tasks of sifting and discovering, scraping and cleaning. Just like the homes, businesses, churches, and schools still standing on all sides of us, we were moving through life with water lines of our own, carrying visible scars of the damage we had sustained, thanks to those stubborn stains that refused to fade.

I pulled my wagon up to the register, feeling like I needed to explain why, in my grief, I was buying basil and not bleach. But I couldn't find the words. They were too ugly to share with a stranger. The pain was too raw to say it out loud.

"I just need some plants right now," I finally said.

"Amen!" said a voice belonging to someone I hadn't realized was standing behind me. A short woman with stringy gray hair had pulled a cart full of plants behind mine. Her clothes were messy, and she had the look of someone who had been dealing with a flooded home, but she too had recognized the need for some dirt under her fingernails and some freshly planted roots.

The girl behind the cash register nodded her agreement. In that moment, three strangers, in the middle of widespread disaster, found hope in new growth.

The next day brought excessive heat and humidity that arrested my body as I stepped outside the house after putting Ruth down for her nap. The air conditioning called to me to come back in, but I needed my garden. It was the only place I was finding any peace. I craved the silence and solitude I found there. Somehow, sifting through my thoughts and the state of my life was easier in that little space.

I kneeled in front of yet another tangled row and thought about the words from Jeremiah again, tossing them around in my brain. I wanted to figure out how to seek God with all of my heart, but I wasn't sure how. I had spent my whole life fine-tuning the art of ignoring Him.

I grabbed my trowel from the box of tools at my side and let my mind wander back to where I was when I got off track. I saw myself at fifteen years old, sitting in the gym of my church, listening to a presentation being made by a team of missionaries who were building a church in an impoverished Central American country. There were probably fifty people in the room, all of whose eyes were glued on the team up front as they explained the unique paths that had led them to that specific role. They described the deplorable conditions in the community where they were based. They talked about their goals and their progress. They were inspiring, so much so that I shifted in my seat.

I watched the faces of the people in the rows beside me. Their hearts were being moved, I could tell. They looked hungry for the Lord's direction.

Meanwhile, my eyes darted from the clock to the door.

I had been an awkward kid. I spent most of my high school years battling frizzy hair and low self-esteem. I never felt I was good enough for the people around me, and I let my concern for how others viewed me dictate my every move.

Because of that, I couldn't fathom how these men and women had accepted a position in life, a job and identity, based on the direction of God—specifically, one that was neither flashy nor safe. In truth, I didn't understand how stuff like that even happened. These were well-educated people who no doubt had their choice of career paths. They could have been doctors or lawyers, or maybe even scientists. Surely they understood that what they had selected for their life was not as solid as some of the other choices on the table.

Did they not long for this beautiful suburban life that surrounded them? We had plenty of clean water and loads of food. We lived in big colonial homes on long, tree-lined, militant-free streets. Didn't any of these comforts entice them?

Furthermore, how did God "guide them" to this job? Had they woken up in the middle of a dream in which an angel told them to pack up their stuff and start spreading the Word in a hostile locale? Did angels visit people anymore? Or did all of that stop in the New Testament? The thought of it was borderline loony to me and incomprehensible.

If God was popping into people's minds in this day and age and telling them to accept what seemed to be a bleak vocation as their calling in life, then maybe I should keep God at arm's reach. It wasn't that I didn't believe He could do it. It was that I feared what His plans might have been for me. I didn't even like airplanes, and I loved to drink water. I figured if I could hide out for a while and sort things out for myself, then maybe God would be satisfied with what I came up with and leave me be. At the very least, maybe He would notice how underwhelming and uninspiring I was and figure I wasn't worth the angel visit.

I had always looked at the prospect of God leading me with apprehension. I understood when people said God had the best possible plans in mind for us, but I was happy with mediocrity so long as I had control.

My prayer life was possibly the best indication of the relationship I sought with God. I didn't ask for direction; I gave directives. My requests were always peppered with the words *fix*, *heal*, and *give*. I wanted God to be my bodyguard, close enough to protect me without taking over to manage the route. If we got lost along the way or took a bad turn, I wanted Him to wait while I regrouped and changed our course. I knew my leadership skills were so-so at best, but I didn't need to conquer the world. I just needed to get by in it.

The evening with the missionaries was just one example of a tension that had been steadily growing between me and my faith. I was trying to get over the hump between the cartoons and praise songs of children's church and an adult commitment to God, and I couldn't quite make the leap. I would sit in church on Sunday mornings and feel like our pastor was preaching about an entirely different God than the one I knew. The word *suffer* was thrown into the mix a lot, and it didn't line up for me. The God I had come to know in Sunday school was all powerful. He could do anything. He could part seas. He could raise people from the dead. If the whole world was in those capable hands, then how could anything bad get in and hurt us? How could God let that happen, if He loved us as much as I believed He did?

I wanted answers. But at fifteen years old, I wanted to fit in more than I wanted those answers. Vocalizing my doubts at that point felt like far too vulnerable an option for a person lacking both courage and confidence.

I started to feel isolated by the reservations swirling in my head. I would show up at church, a place I had once felt so welcome, and feel like an outsider, an imposter who didn't deserve to be there—a harsh and unsettling identity crisis for a young girl who desperately needed grounding.

Looking back, I now know the devil "prowls around like a roaring lion, looking for someone to devour" (1 Peter 5:8). And I made easy prey. I ran away from my home in the church, away from the feelings of inadequacy swallowing me up, and away from God. It wasn't that I had stopped believing in Him. I just felt like a lone skeptic in a community of otherwise strong believers, a weak link threatening to bring down a sturdy structure. I didn't belong.

I stood up and surveyed the now clear plot in front of me. All the weeds had been extracted. My plants were no longer lost behind a mass of overgrowth.

As I studied the freshly tilled earth, I pictured the bedroom in my parents' house that I had left behind when I moved to college. I could still see the index cards adorned with scriptures that lined my walls in that room. I left them there when I moved out, and I left my relationship with God there with them.

When I moved to Boston to attend college, I grew, but not with the Lord. I wanted space from my church and a break from the questions that swirled in my head about God and suffering and being led.

Downtown Boston was rich in culture but lacking in Christianity, and I embraced that. My friends and I drank beer and argued over baseball games. We didn't try to work out deep-rooted questions of faith.

Still, the city cultivated an important part of my identity. It was a temporary home where I found my inspiration and my confidence. While there, I learned to embrace my personality instead of trying to adapt it to adhere to the narrow social confines of my small town. I bought a flat iron to tame the frizz and learned to love my quirkiness. I built friendships with people who loved those quirks too. I was being who I was, not who I thought I had to be, and it was a stark and refreshing contrast to my life in the suburbs.

Six years later, when I decided to move to Louisiana with Brad, I felt God calling me home. I would drive by churches and picture myself going inside. I would browse the websites of congregations in the same way some people browse for shoes. But I seldom went inside those churches, and when I did find myself stepping through their doors, I stayed noncommittal. I didn't want to relent on the things I thought were unreasonable about Christianity, and I didn't want to get too engaged and have that exposed. I was like an immature child who loved her parents but didn't want to hear everything they had to say. I wanted to have a relationship with God, but I wanted to build it on my own terms.

I found a niche for myself in the non-church-going crowd. There, I could outwardly proclaim Christianity as my faith but not see that as reason enough to commit my day-to-day life to God and His work on earth. I stayed at home on Sundays, tending to my yard rather than my soul.

I am a procrastinator. I put things off I don't want to deal with, like folding the laundry, emptying the dishwasher, and sorting out disagreements I have with God. I thought if I could remain in the doorway, on the threshold of the church, without acknowledging my doubts and fears, then I could be a Christian from the safety of the shadows. I could pick and choose what I was comfortable hearing and disregard the rest without anyone noticing or calling me out for it.

I stood up and loosened the dirt from the shovel, considering things a bit further.

Maybe the threshold of the church wasn't as safe as I had thought it was. Maybe the threshold was my problem. It was a wedge, a division, that I laid down to separate myself from God, and now I didn't know how to get past it and be close to Him. Would He even let me close? Or was the damage I had inflicted on our relationship too deep?

I played the words from Jeremiah back through my head one more time: "Then you will call on me and come and pray to me, and I will listen to you. You will seek me and find me when you seek me with all your heart."

This time, I remembered their context. He still wanted the Israelites when they arrived in Babylon. Of course He still wanted me.

Chapter 6

THE NEXT DAY, I herded Ruth to the garden bright and early. I was anxious to get back to the comfort of that space, to the peace and silence it offered, and to revisit where my thoughts had left off the day before.

I knew God would take me back. But how? How could I find Him? What was the appropriate level of seeking, and what did that seeking look like? More importantly, how in the world was He going to go about fixing things for me? Could He flip a switch, like a parted sea, and let me cruise past all this? Would He give me a map? I was a visual learner. A crafty illustration would be perfect. Maybe He could direct me with colorful icons and a few arrows. That would do the trick.

I tossed the map idea God's way, wondering if He would send one back with expedited delivery. I was in a bind, after all.

Nothing happened.

Well, maybe God worked in bullet points. A list would be fantastic—"Ten Steps to a Restored Soul." I could work with that too.

Still, none of it seemed right.

I looked down at the row in front of me. It

was empty and needed something planted in it. *Sunflowers*, I thought with a smile. Sunflowers can be planted in August.

I went into my gardening shed and started rifling through the seeds I kept stacked in a box on the first shelf. Tomatoes, no. Peppers, no. Cucumbers? Absolutely not.

I forgot about my quest for sunflower seeds when my fingers landed on a thick packet of mustard seeds. Those are always the biggest bag of seeds I have. They're my go-to choice for leafy greens, so easy and dependable. All the others come with long lists of "ifs" and "buts" that I can never seem to get right, but mustard seeds just grow. They don't care if you're a mediocre gardener. They don't even need you.

I took one of the mustard seeds out of the bag and rolled it in my fingers, perfectly round and no bigger than the period at the end of a sentence. The tiny but tenacious mustard seed.

I smiled, remembering the parable Jesus told about mustard seeds and mountains. I always loved how He chose to use plants and farming in His analogies. He knew how closely related our souls are to the fundamentals of cultivation. We need to build good foundations for both our plants and our souls. We need to keep them from getting cluttered. We need to feed them appropriately. We need to encourage the good growth and thwart the bad.

I played the words of Jesus in my head, still rolling the seed in my fingers:

> "Truly I tell you, if you have faith as small as a mustard seed, you can say to this mountain, 'Move from here to there,' and it will move. Nothing will be impossible for you."
>
> —MATTHEW 17:20, NIV

Then I started to tally all the things that were wrong within my soul. I was terrified. My heart was broken. I was worried about the future of my community and the lives of my neighbors. I was confused, angry, and tormented by guilt. I wondered if these emotions, when combined, could be deemed a mountain. They felt mountain-ish.

There aren't many things that can make you feel as small and ill-equipped as standing at the foot of a mountain. Few people can up and climb a mountain at a moment's notice. It requires patience and knowledge and commitment and preparation—even more so in biblical times, when there were no fancy shoes or Clif Bars or gondolas to take you through a mountain pass. Maybe what I was in for would be much the same.

Looking at the seed, I saw myself. It symbolized the tiny fragment of faith I still had left after all the years I'd spent wandering, separating myself from God.

Jesus had been clear. He didn't need faith the size of pumpkin seed. Small was enough. Small would get me started.

Suddenly I felt like I needed to write these

thoughts down. Maybe doing so would help anchor my mind in some way.

I walked into the house and searched for the spiral notebooks that housed the three unfinished books that had been sitting on the back shelf of my life. I grabbed one of them and flipped to a clean sheet of paper. Then I reached for my Bible and turned to the book of Matthew and wrote down each word of the verse about the mustard seed at the top of a blank page. I felt like a kid again, carefully writing out each line.

Below the verse, I made my own list of bullet points. My mountain. I wrote:

- Scared
- Confused
- Sad
- Worried
- Guilty
- Angry

There was nothing inspiring about this list. It lacked the colorful run-on sentences that typically adorned my work. It was short and concise; I am not. There was no rich story line laid out with excessive detail. But somehow, I felt God loving it.

The peace that filled my soul at the sight of those words on paper felt odd to me. In years past, my writing had been a source of unrest. I enjoyed writing, and often words flowed through me in such a way that it felt like one of the most natural things for me to do. But I often struggled to find the purpose in it. What was I writing for? Occasionally I dropped depth into my words, but for the most part, my writing had always been funny but shallow.

My response to that restlessness had been to stop writing completely. I stacked my notebooks up, stored my computer on a back shelf, and walked away, in pursuit of activities that had purposes I understood and outcomes I could see.

In this moment, staring at my black letters on the notebook's thin blue lines, something started to come into focus for me. It felt a bit like purpose.

Still, it was hard to understand why I felt peace in the purpose of something that seemed insignificant. I had written better stuff. This sheet of paper held words I had plucked from the Bible and a few one-word bullet points. This was not good writing. This was a list.

Nevertheless, something about it felt unmistakably right. I set the notebook aside, wondering if more would come another day.

The next morning, I stood in the kitchen, drinking my coffee and staring at the notebook on the counter. I kept playing with the verse in my head. *Move the mountain. Nothing is impossible. Mountain, move. Relocate mountain, please.*

How do you move a mountain, anyway? That's a big task.

I stared at the paper and tried to picture it happening, like the slow change of backdrops you see while watching a grade-school play, everything inching off the stage and then, suddenly, a new landscape is in front of you. Mountain gone.

After a while, I set the notebook aside and started scrolling through my newsfeed. It was time to get back to the business of helping my neighbors. We needed books, canned food, cleaning supplies, homewares, and clothing. I could help with all of that. I needed to help with all of that.

But I looked at my garden longingly. I wanted to put my community back together as badly as I wanted to put myself back together, but it all felt so big. Maybe I would be more helpful to everyone else if I, myself, was whole.

Was there a way to just help from home?

I had found a little block of safety in that small square of earth outside my kitchen window. I didn't want to go back down the road. I didn't want to drive past all the destruction. I didn't want to face any of it until I felt confident enough to face what was before me in my own life and in my own heart.

I tried to talk my way out of helping but instead found my fingers commenting on each post and committing to bring things where they needed to go. I had to. I felt a nudge in the pit of my soul. It was steady and firm. No voice accompanied it, but it directed me nonetheless. Was God a nudger?

I thrust myself into the movement of repair, the citywide effort to find and fill the needs of the hundreds of thousands of people and animals who had absolutely nothing. The chaos was big, but I was amazed and inspired by the determination of our community. We were not going to back down from this event. We were going to fight it and demand we not be broken by it.

I charged through, and every single time I felt like stopping, I pictured the shoes of the people all around me. They were soggy and muddy shoes. They held shaking feet that fled in boats from water that proved unexpected and unforgiving. They were stacked in rows at shelters, often the only two things some feet had left. They were going home to houses that had been destroyed or damaged. They were covered in the dust and dirt of demolition. If they were lucky, they were being coated with the plaster and paint of repair. Too many of those shoes had walked through dark and damp woods, searching for pets in vain. They had ventured down roads and collected destroyed belongings. Their soles were wearing out, and their colors were fading, but they were still moving, because they had no other choice.

A few weeks later, I stood in the kitchen, exhausted. I was behind on everything. The house was a mess.

The yard was a mess. I hadn't been down to our barn once since we had buried the horses. I couldn't figure out where I was going or if I was going anywhere at all.

Just then, my phone rang. It was Brad. He had found an opening for Ruth in a swim lesson in Baton Rouge, and it started that day. He thought it would be nice for both of us to get involved with something new and fun, and I knew he was right. I hung up the phone, smiling at my sweet husband, who was looking for things to fill the void he knew burned in our hearts.

Later that day, we showed up at the swim school. My brave little girl beamed up at me, wearing her brand-new goggles, and I grinned. She did need a distraction.

It felt strange to be in Baton Rouge, though. Everything seemed normal. None of this area had flooded, and it felt like an odd release from the prison we had left in our town, a prison of gutted homes and debris piles.

Parents weren't allowed in the pool area, so we lined up along the outside of the fence to watch from a distance. We laughed at the kids and exchanged small talk about the summer heat.

Inevitably, the conversation led to the flood. No one was untouched by it, even if the water never rose on their home or in their neighborhood.

I noticed the woman next to me had eyes that were tired like mine. We carried the same stature, standing upright because we had to but still very much on our knees. My heart dropped when she told us her home of forty-five years had filled with three feet of murky water. I watched the creases in her sweet eyes swell as she repeated the words not for emphasis or for us, but for herself. "Forty-five years," she said. She was still trying to make sense of it.

Courage laced with despair coated each word. My heart burned at the sound of her regret. She was speaking to my soul. I had repeated my own river data in my head again and again, wondering if I could make sense of it if I said it enough times. I knew, as those words slipped off of her lips, that she could still feel the terror.

She bit her lip, an expression somewhere between anger and grief on her face. She told us about her mother's china cabinet.

"She had only just passed," the woman said, staring up at the sky. "We had to drag the cabinet out to the curb like a piece of trash. There was no saving it."

She shook her head and then looked up, full-blown mad.

"It was bad enough to have to do that," she continued, "but then I looked outside and saw looters in broad daylight sifting through the garbage bags I had only just filled with all my possessions—my pictures, my clothes, everything. They were ripping the bags apart and throwing the contents all over the yard."

She shook her head again, trying to fight the anger but also maybe trying to find the words.

"Then they knocked that china cabinet down like a piece of junk and broke its glass all over the road," she said.

I started to cry as I played the scene out in my head. The whole thing was cruel. Demeaning. The boundaries between us had decayed. Nothing was off limits.

She stared into the distance like I often do when I'm thinking and then shook her head slowly. "So back we went, exhausted, and bagged it all up again—and, you know, with most of it, it's really okay. I can close my eyes and still see my wedding day. I don't need the pictures. Most of it was just stuff. The only thing that gets me were the scrapbooks I had made that summer with my grandkids. They were fresh memories. They had things in them that couldn't be replaced, and I wasn't ready to lose them."

The conversation kept flowing. We talked about insurance claims and the holding pattern she and her husband were in while they waited to see if the government would require them to lift their house before fixing it. Lifting their home would be an expense that almost exceeded its value, and it wasn't something they were prepared to pay for in retirement.

When the swim lesson was over, Ruth and I got into the car. But as I shifted it into drive, I felt a new wave of hopelessness close in on me. My soul was like a thirsty tree, its roots drying up and leaves falling. Soon the tree would have no foliage, and any observer would be left to wonder if it was going to come back in the next season or at all.

Every day I felt a little more drained. There was too much wrong. What did the future of our community look like? This woman was just one of hundreds of thousands who were taken out by this storm. What was going to become of us? How would we bounce back?

I stopped at a red light and rubbed my forehead with the palm of my hand. This was too big.

When I got off the interstate, I braced myself for the journey through the roads that led back home. Our house is twenty miles from the exit, and on that drive, I passed only five homes that did not flood.

There was no escape from the memories. Maybe we should have stayed in our garden after all.

I got stuck behind a debris removal truck about ten miles south of our house. I watched the giant claw grab at the mound of furniture, clothing, appliances, and insulation, and I thought about my new friend from swim lessons, how she had shook with anger and fought back tears when she talked about her debris pile and the looters. I understood how she felt beaten down by a world she had trusted.

Then I felt a nudge. She needed something.

But I felt a little indignant. Surely God knew I could not fix this woman's problems. They were big and outside of my wheelhouse. I could not slip her a check for the money she needed to lift her house above the flood line. I could not refurbish her mother's china cabinet. I could not replace her wedding pictures. I could not help refurnish her home, and I was in no position to foot the bill to restore it.

I started to get angry. This was nonsense. When were we going to shift gears and stop making me feel worse? I didn't think I could continue to exist under the weight of the problems that surrounded me. I felt as if mine were enough to break me. I didn't want any more hopeless situations to worry about. All I wanted was to go home and not come back out until I could live in a world that wasn't a constant reminder of that night on the boat.

I didn't even care about being fixed anymore. I just wanted a break. I wanted to be alone. Just send a cave.

That night, I couldn't shake the woman from my mind. She filled my prayers when my words said something different. I realized that while I couldn't heal her situation, maybe I could do something to nourish her soul.

The scrapbooks. So simple, yet so meaningful. When your house floods, you need to think about replacing your clothing, your footwear, and your car. You purchase flooring, furniture, drywall, and paint. But those things heal structures, not souls. I knew a scrapbook wouldn't fix her, but maybe it would make her feel acknowledged in this sea of suffering in which we were all treading water.

The next morning, I went to the local craft store and got a card and a gift certificate. When I met up with her at swim lessons later that day, tears filled her eyes as she read the card.

"Thank you," she said, hugging me. "Thank you so much."

I loved that I had been able to find what I thought was a fitting way to show her love amid such a devastating situation. Still, as I stood there in the sweltering heat, I couldn't help but wonder how many other people were suffering in solitude without the hope of even the smallest gesture to soothe their waterlogged souls.

Every side street told its own story. Families who lived in tents because they had nowhere else to stay. Single moms who lost their cars and whose places of employment also flooded, making a paycheck-by-paycheck life downright terrifying. People who had spent their lifetimes building businesses, only to see those businesses inundated with water at the same time their homes flooded, neither benefiting from insurance because they were outside what had been determined to be official flood zones.

We were all waiting in line, all in desperate need of God's attention and healing, but the line wasn't moving. Was it backlogged, just like the water had been?

I felt frustrated that my first experience of prayerfully seeking God's direction was leaving me more drained and exposing more hopelessness, rather than restoring the hope I had lost.

On the way home, we hit traffic from the debris removal trucks again, but this time it happened in front of a horse farm. I watched Ruth's eyes in the rearview mirror. She studied the grazing animals intently.

After a few seconds, she looked at me with red eyes and said, "Mommy, why Jacky had to go with Jesus?"

This was a final blow for the day.

"I am really not sure, my baby," I said.

"Will he ever come back to my house?" She was almost whimpering, but her voice still held hints of hope.

"No, baby. He isn't going to be able to do that."

As she processed the magnitude of that answer, she looked down at her little fingers, pressing them against each other in a deliberate rhythm, maybe willing her own kind of strength from it.

After a few minutes, she looked me square in the eyes and said, "It's not fair. Jacky needs me. I need Jacky."

I gripped my steering wheel, willing myself to get us home safely but feeling like I might shut down. Tears poured from my eyes, making it impossible to see the road. I wiped my face and felt my skin burn.

Ruth was a few months shy of her third birthday. Her biggest concern should have been how to weasel her way out of nap time or which crayons are best for coloring within the lines. She should have been entrenched in a world of fairy tales. Instead, she had to wake up to drowned pets, water that nearly engulfed her home, and a leveled community.

I didn't recognize my life. I had been careful to do everything right for this precious little person. I had picked the best foods, bought the best toys, and followed the best sleep practices. I had read books on how to parent and how to raise a good child. I had prepared in every way I thought possible. But I was not prepared for dealing with this.

I was so angry I couldn't shield her from this pain. It broke me, knowing I couldn't prevent this from happening to her. I had filtered everything I could—books, movies, music—careful to pick messages that relayed light and happiness, not evil or darkness. But I could not filter this.

I wanted to carry this burden for her, but that wasn't an option. I could not cover her eyes, nor could I cushion her heart.

I was exhausted by the endless delivery runs. I was tired of helping other people. I was ready to focus on my own disasters at home. I wanted a nudge-free day to tend to myself.

But each time the nudge-free day didn't come, I pictured the cartoon faces of the characters from the storybook version of the account of the widow and

Elijah I had read as a child. Elijah was a prophet who was led by God to a widow and was told she would feed him. All the widow had left was a little bit of oil and a little bit of flour. But she had faith in God and shared what she had, despite her reservations, and that small bit never ran out until the drought in the area passed.

I imagined the cartoon figures exchanging flour and oil and reminded myself to have faith in the fact that God doesn't ever let us run out. But I wasn't smiling like the woman in the cartoon picture. I was running on fumes.

Maybe that story isn't applicable here, I thought. Maybe I had nothing in common with the widow besides the fact that we were both girls. Maybe I could run out. Maybe I was running out in this very moment. Perhaps it was time to tap out on this nudge business and regroup, to listen to myself for a bit, until I felt stronger and more capable to handle the world around me.

I didn't know what to do with myself as I pulled into our driveway and got out to retrieve our mail at the end of the drive. When I hopped back into the car, I let my defenses down and sat there crying. I cried harder than I had ever cried in my life. I cried for the horses. I cried for Ruth. I cried for my friend at swim lessons and for every other person with a story like hers. I cried for our town. I cried for myself.

Ruth watched silently from the back seat. I wanted

so badly to do better for her. I didn't want to let her down, but I was falling to pieces.

Maybe I was wrong about more than just the connection to the widow with Elijah. Maybe I was wrong about everything. Maybe the verses from Jeremiah had nothing to do with me. Maybe God's arms were not outstretched for me anymore. There were more people living these days. Maybe His criteria for wanderers had become more stringent.

I had, admittedly, been pretty adamant about not listening to Him. Maybe God was tired of my lack of obedience. Maybe I hadn't made the cut. Or maybe the story wasn't intended for comparison. Maybe my imagination was too big for this one. Maybe a story is just a story.

Maybe I wasn't even at mustard-seed status. Maybe I was more like a lettuce seed, narrow and prone to wilting. Or a tomato seed, tiny and a complete pain to deal with. If that was so, was my mountain permanent?

I put the car in drive and rolled down the remainder of the driveway in silent contemplation.

Before I got out of the car, I sifted through the coupons and catalogs. Then my fingers came to rest on not one, but two small envelopes. Two letters.

The first one was addressed with handwriting I recognized, perfect penmanship I had known my whole life. It felt like home just to look at it. It was a cursive hand I'd come to recognize on birthday cards, recipes, postcards, and Christmas cards—my grandmother's sister's handwriting. She was the last remaining matriarch of a family that had once been well supported by elders. Years ago, she had opened her arms to me when I had no grandparents left to hug and no old, wise ears left to listen. She was my pen pal, my friend, my family, and an anchor to my roots. She had her own people to worry about, but she always made space for me too. And here she was now, reaching out to me when I desperately needed her.

I opened the envelope and cried as I read her words, each letter she wrote now shaky. We had agreed years ago that typing was better for her aching hands, but she had struggled to encourage me in this letter with each painful stroke of her pen.

She included a generous gift and told me to use it to replace some of what I lost or to put it toward the continued recovery efforts in my community. I was blown away.

The second letter was addressed with handwriting I did not recognize but carried a return address for a name I did—a name just as familiar to me as those glossy white pews, those crimson cushions, that plush gray carpet, those boxwoods. The woman who sent this second letter was part of the community that was my family. She was a prayer warrior still standing, and she was writing to tell me she was still lifting me up in her prayers that day. She included a generous gift, as well, that she hoped would help us to recover. I couldn't believe it.

These women were God's vessels. They had

lifetimes behind them of being His hands and His feet. There were no identifiers stronger for either one of them than their place in God's arsenal of tools. Their lives were a witness to that.

Goose bumps traveled down my arms. The timing of it. The power of it. It was all so deliberate and perfectly executed.

These two letters did so much to open my eyes to who God is. He showed me love and compassion when I was feeling some pretty intense doubt. Instead of addressing my failure to trust Him, He acknowledged my struggle with a bold and definite gesture, but He did so in a way that encouraged me to step outside myself and study the bigger picture circling around me—the picture of how He gets His work done. He does it through an intricate network of people who follow nudges with faith that they will be sustained along the way. He does it through obedience.

My nudges weren't a burden. They were an invitation to participate in something much bigger than myself.

I grabbed Ruth from the car and climbed the stairs to the house. As I put her down, I stood in silent contemplation. My mind was completely blown.

That evening, I sat in my living room, struggling to find the words to thank those two women. How could I possibly convey how perfect their gestures were for a girl who was, in that very moment, considering tapping out on her relationship with God?

As I blanked on where to start, I noticed my Bible on the table behind me and reached for it. I flipped to 1 Kings 17 and reread the story of Elijah and the widow, noting that the cartoon version had been toned down considerably. The widow was dying of starvation at the point the story started. When Elijah came to her, she was about to prepare what she thought would be her last meal with her son before they both… tapped out. Forever.

I set my Bible down, knowing I had learned a lot that afternoon, not the least of which was that those old tales I loved so much were not just stories. They were guides, just as I had always believed. They were just as much for me as they were for the people who had written them. Times have changed, yes, but God hasn't. He's still working, and His work is still done by obedient people who trust Him.

I could be a dead end, or I could be a vessel. It was my choice.

A few weeks later, I stood in my driveway as a giant cargo van full of donations backed into my carport. My cousins in Massachusetts had been hard at work collecting supplies, and this van held the fruits of their labors.

I opened the van's back door and was speechless at the sight that greeted me: a mountain of cleaning products, school supplies, toiletries, and clothes. It was a dream come true.

The following day, I loaded a few bags full of supplies into the back of my car and buckled Ruth into her car seat. Just as I was about to pull down the road, I stopped and opened the music app on my phone.

"Why aren't we going?" Ruth asked.

"I just need one second," I replied, scrolling through the list of songs. "I need something first."

"What?" she asked, confused.

I paused for a moment, slightly confused myself. What did I need?

"I think... I think I need some hymns," I said, now scrolling through a long list of different versions of "Trust and Obey" that had popped up in response to my search. I found a folksy band that had recorded that song and several of my other favorites, and I downloaded them all.

"What's a hymn?" Ruth asked, a quizzical look on her face.

"You'll see—and you're going to love them, just like your mama does."

I turned the first song up with a smile. The melody filled my car, and I could feel myself sinking down into my roots—the roots that I knew, without a doubt, were the answer to surviving this situation.

I thought about my cousins and their fund-raising efforts. They had banded together across three towns and collected all those items. Then my cousin Jessie's husband, Tim, had packed up his van and drove down by himself with more donations and had even volunteered, gutting houses while his kids stayed home and set up a lemonade stand with a giant sign that read "Lemonade for Louisiana."

My heart was heavy, but the light shining from way up north lifted me. I was grateful for the kindness and compassion being shown by my sweet family and their neighbors. I had been caught in the middle of a tug-of-war between hope and hopelessness. Thanks to them, on that day, hope was winning.

I passed my neighbor's stately white home and thought of him, as I often did. I could still see his sad eyes on the day after the flood, when I had met him on the street. An enormous Dumpster blocked the driveway to his house. A large Oriental rug draped the railing of the wraparound porch, the stairs of which were still stuck in the wood line. I said a prayer for him as I rounded the bend. I wondered if he had found hope of his own.

I wasn't sure where I was going that day. The bags I had made up were full of basic necessities: toiletries, food, toilet paper, paper towels, and cleaning supplies.

I felt a nudge toward a neighborhood I often thought about. We had driven past it right after the flood, and its future had looked the bleakest to me. From the main road, I had seen people walking out of the neighborhood carrying garbage bags of possessions, their pant legs rolled up but still soaked with muddy water. At the front of the neighborhood, about fifteen cars were piled on top of each other, older sedans that probably weren't much to begin with, but the water had finished them off completely. By the looks of things, water had come close to the roofs of the houses in this neighborhood, and a few small boats were still tied to power poles by the front of the road.

In truth, I didn't want to drive through this neighborhood on that day—or on any other day. There are certain neighborhoods you just don't drive through, and this was one of them. I thought about taking my nudge and moving it to the back seat of my brain.

There had to be a better, safer place to go. Maybe I could happen upon someone who needed these bags of goods before I got to that street. Then that would be not so much the ignoring of a nudge but an unfortunate nudge diversion.

Considering I had to drive thirty minutes to get there and would not pass a single house that hadn't flooded along the way, it shouldn't have been hard to find someone else to whom I could give the stuff. But I didn't. Instead, I found myself at the entrance to the neighborhood, gripping my steering wheel and wondering what on earth I was doing.

At first, the place looked entirely abandoned. The houses, and even most of the trees, were light tan, still coated from dried river mud up to the tips of their roofs. The colors, or lack thereof, made it almost look like a desert. A few bikes and toys hung suspended in trees. Lawn chairs and tables had washed into the corner edge of fences. The air smelled rank with mold. Many of the houses' front doors hung open, possibly untouched since the night their inhabitants had fled for their lives a month earlier.

I shivered at the contrast between the dull sight and my shiny black car.

I passed a house with two disheveled Hondas out front and noticed a guy crouched behind a blown-out bay window. His eyes looked vacant as they followed my car rolling by. I felt no friendly vibes.

Chills ran down my back. I needed to get out of there. Nudge mistaken.

Then I felt a rush of confidence and assurance nudging me to stay. But I was still too wounded to trust anything other than the fear building inside of me. I searched for a spot to turn around.

I saw a woman sweeping mud off the door frame of a house two doors down. She wore dingy sweatpants, her shoulders hunched over her tiny frame. She couldn't have been much older than me, but her face and body seemed aged by the task ahead of her.

When I pulled up in front of the house, her facial expression conveyed a mixture of confusion and aggravation. I rolled my window down, still terrified but knowing I needed to power through, and told her I had food and some cleaning supplies. Would she like some?

She paused for a second, and then her face softened.

I could have sworn she exhaled audibly. I hopped out of my car and handed her several bags of supplies. As I was turning back to my car, she hugged me.

While I sat at the light to turn out of the neighborhood, I processed what I had just seen. It was unsettling to see so much devastation so close to my home. At the same time, a tiny bit of progress had been made on that day for that one woman on that one disaster of a street. It was a small thing in the middle of a big mess, but it was still something. And something, even something small, is far better than nothing.

Maybe hope doesn't always come in huge packages. Maybe all hope needs is two legs and a willingness to follow nudges when we can.

As I thought on that, I saw six men in hazmat suits walk out of a home in front of me. They carried moldy construction debris and hoisted it onto the growing pile stacked high by the road. I spied two tattered couches, yellow-green cabinets, a blue toilet and pile of blue tile, brown shag carpet, and a few boxes of Christmas ornaments.

A large truck sat in the driveway, hitched to a trailer with the name of a well-known church painted on its side. These church crews were becoming as familiar a sight in our community as the water lines and debris piles. Some churches were local, and some were from far-off places. Some crews were big, and others small. All of them whittled away at the lists of homes that needed to be gutted, lists full of names of people who needed hope. Every member of the crew followed nudges of their own, powered by the generosity of the church and its members. God's house creating hope in numbers.

As the last hymn on my new soundtrack played, the pause after its conclusion made me think of one of my favorite pauses in a church service—the part where the congregation is suspended in silence between the offertory hymn and one of the most commanding hymns of all.

I stared past the red light and pictured the bright red carpet that lines the aisle of my old church home. I could hear the creaking of the ushers' feet on the wood floor beneath its plush surface as they marched toward the pulpit with brass plates in hand. Then I could hear the congregation stand and join voices for the Doxology:

> Praise God, from whom all blessings flow;
> Praise Him, all creatures here below;
> Praise Him above, ye heavenly host;
> Praise Father, Son, and Holy Ghost.

Those words had never been more fitting than in that exact moment. Our blessings, *flowing*.

I thought about all of us, how we'd spent our lifetimes filling up homes and other structures with many things. Some brought us sustenance, while others brought us comfort and joy. We clung to all of them, picking and choosing each item that passed through our doors. We had stored up, we had built, we had cherished, and we had found pride. To varying degrees, we had believed there was some level of control in the flow of things into and out of our homes.

Then the water had flowed through those structures and claimed what it did. We had watched it all flow out, helpless to stop it or save anything from the current.

But then generosity flowed toward us in various forms—notes, letters, gifts, hands, feet, and hope. Somewhere in it all, we had gone from being built up by our own devices to being rebuilt by the love and generosity of others, by God's power.

And nothing, not even the disaster before us these days, was too big for God. He moves His vessels to "do His good will," as the hymn "Trust and Obey" aptly notes. He sees to it that miracles happen around us, even in the middle of widespread destruction. Even when hope seems out of reach.

I placed my head on the back of my seat and thought about it some more. One tiny, untrained voice may sound weak in the middle of an empty sanctuary, but two hundred voices can create electricity and power when they join together and sing.

Not everything has to be big on its own. Small gestures, combined, can move mountains.

Chapter 7

I had spent weeks hoping for a break from the nudges that continued to pull me from home, but now I would have done anything to go back to them. Instead, I stood in the entrance to our barn. Motionless, I studied the extent of the damage.

I didn't have it in me.

This structure felt like a gravestone. A black mark on the story of my life. A place where my dreams had lived and then died. I didn't want to look at it, much less fix it. So it had sat, frozen in time and coated in thick, dried-up river mud.

The water hadn't even been kind enough to leave the ground in place. The barn sat on its footings, surrounded by washed-out silt. Every board had busted under the pressure of the current. Branches and twigs hung in the rafters. Piles of leaves and downed trees lay on top of the fence. This barn was just as beaten and broken as I was.

I stared up at it, my hands on my hips, wondering if the best thing, for it and for me, would be to light a match on it and let it burn. Could I wipe out all the memories it stood for if I did that?

I thought back to a dark November evening nearly two years before. I could see myself sitting in the kitchen of this brand-new house, running low on energy. We had purchased the house a few weeks earlier, and on that Friday night, an air mattress lay on the floor of our new bedroom and a Pack 'n Play was set up in Ruth's new room.

I had spent the day unloading a trailer full of furniture and boxes. I'd painted walls and then taken the two-hour round trip back to our old house to feed the horses and stock up on clean pants for a toddler who had decided there was too much chaos in this week to be potty trained. I was exhausted with the back-and-forth trips between the houses. Each new box we brought over held items that didn't seem to have a place in this new and smaller home, and several weekends of work lay between us and our horses being able to move there, which meant several more weeks of twice-daily trips to and from. There was so much to do, and I wasn't sure there was enough in us to get started, much less finish.

That evening, things were falling apart, as they so often do for families with little ones as the nighttime hours roll in. I had finished painting a half hour earlier, and dinner had not been ready in time for the smallest belly in the bunch. I was trying to comfort her while I cooked, but I didn't have any of the right stuff to make her feel at home and settle down. We were just two girls standing in a house that wasn't yet our home, surrounded by boxes and feeling out of sorts about the whole deal.

I wondered if we had made the right decision. I

just wanted to sit down somewhere and be at home for a second, but home was neither here nor there. I was standing in the kitchen with my daughter in one arm, cleaning the only pot I had unpacked with the other arm, and staring out of the window above the sink, taking note of what this new place looked like after dark. It was the first night we had spent there, and I was amazed at how quickly the pitch-black sky had settled in once the sun had set over the pond at the bottom of the hill below the house.

We need lights, I thought. *Lots and lots of lights*.

Then, as the weight of that moment and the events of the day overwhelmed me, Brad pulled into the long driveway. The headlights of his big white Ford F-250 broke through the night sky and illuminated the wraparound porch that encompassed our new house.

He was hauling a trailer full of answers to my day's prayers: a rented auger, a pallet of concrete, and enough 4x4s to make a pasture out of the field that adjoined the structure that would be our barn.

I breathed a sigh of relief at the sight of him. He was still wearing dress pants and a button-down shirt from the day of work he had put in before he'd started gathering up all these supplies that evening. He was lighting up the dark that had been threatening my outlook only moments before, my can-doer of a husband, who always had a way of solving my problems and settling my worried soul. He was the engine of our family that kept running when I started to shut down.

Brad built me a big, beautiful fence that weekend, then two stalls the weekend after that. True to the engineer in him, he drew out plans, made lists, dug holes, set posts, built walls, and made that shell of a building look like a home in an unfamiliar place.

Until that terrible night in August, this barn had brought me immense joy. Every day I had set foot in it, I had thought about how God had blessed me in my life. Blessed me with a husband who was willing to rebuild the inside of not one, but two barns in less than ten years of marriage. The type of man who builds fences for me everywhere we move. The man who makes my dreams come true—dreams that are not his own.

I stood looking at the barn post-flood, surveying the damage and trying to decide its fate, and started to realize the barn hadn't been taken from me. The stack of memories from those first few weekends we lived here were intact: the one of the two of us taking a selfie with the first post we set between those two stalls; the one of Ruth holding a string line; the funny one of my parents riding on a trailer full of lumber; Brad holding Ruth and showing her how to work a level; the first pizza party with Matt and Mynde after a long day of work.

Not one of those memories was tainted. I could

choose to run away from this building and abandon those memories in a pile of rubble along with everything else—or I could put up a fight.

I wasn't sure how much fight I had in me, but looking at Ruth, who was standing beside me, I found myself willing to try. I just needed some words. I needed the Bible. I didn't have one on me, so I settled for my phone. I grabbed it and googled "scripture comfort," then scrolled through the suggestions that popped up on my screen. So many good words, but not *the* words I needed.

I couldn't be told how to find fight. I needed to be shown. So I tried again, using my best description for myself as my keywords: "scripture broken."

Halfway down the screen, my eyes rested on Psalm 34:

> The Lord is near to the brokenhearted
> And saves those who are crushed in spirit.
>
> Many are the afflictions of the righteous,
> But the Lord delivers him out of them all.
> He keeps all his bones,
> Not one of them is broken.
>
> —Psalm 34:18–20, nasb

I rested what felt like a broken head on the back of a broken board in my broken barn and let those words sink in. God hears me. He will deliver me out of this. I am not in this dark and sad place for good, and I am not alone. He is near to me. My favorite part, though, was this: "He keeps all his bones, not one of them is broken." In that moment, in my heart, it didn't seem like those words were talking about broken bones. It felt like they referenced permanent damage, lasting harm, irreversible injury.

Broken bones can be major. They hurt, and they can be sore even after they heal. Oftentimes you are not as good at the same things afterward as you were beforehand. But back then, when this psalm was written? Broken bones may have meant being maimed for the rest of your life. They didn't have fancy surgeons or cutting-edge bone-fixing technologies back then. In David's time, broken bones were game changers.

This passage encouraged me by telling me my crushed spirit would not be equivalent to such an injury. I was not irreversibly harmed. I would move on from this, changed but not permanently damaged. How about that? Losses surrounded me, and my wounds may have yet to be healed, but an end would come if I kept my head lifted toward Him.

I stood up, repeating the verse in my head. Each time I ran the words through my mind, I felt a little more defiant toward my sorrow. The Lord was near me. I shouldn't feel defeated, because I couldn't be defeated.

I could feel something igniting in my soul, a spark of that fire my dad had tried to find in me a few weeks before, the part of me that was determined to dust myself off from this fall and start reclaiming what I could from this storm.

I did not need to drag my feet through life, wondering if this had crushed me for another minute. This scripture reminded me it could not have crushed me. My bones would not be broken. I was just wounded for now, like the barn, a shell of something we both once were.

I knew something, though, and that was that this structure before me had been in this state when we found it. My stack of pictures from November reminded me God had used love to build it into something better. It was through love that an abandoned woodworking shed was converted into a place full of joy. I just needed to show it some love one more time and do it all again.

I picked up a rake and began lifting the leaves from the fence. Tears rolled down my face as I guided a downed branch through the hole where Jack had been stuck. Ruth looked up from her coloring and asked why I was crying. The poor thing had to be sick of my tears. This time, though, when she asked, I felt my shoulders straighten up. I sensed my old self coming back to the weakened frame that was my body, a more confident version of myself banging on the door of my soul, looking to come back in.

I gazed at Ruth through my tear-filled eyes and responded, "I think it's about time we fixed this place, baby. What do you think?"

She nodded, then dropped her crayons, grabbed

her rake, and joined me. She was just as sick of all of this as I was.

Together, we made our way down the fence line, revealing more of what once was with each pile of leaves we pulled back. It was all still under there, hidden beneath the debris.

When we reset each post, I was amazed to find the nails that had once held the wires to the wood. They were sitting on the ground, directly in front of the posts from which they had detached. I held one of the nails in my hand and stared at it indignantly. With so much chaos caused by the water, so much random stuff strewn everywhere, debris from six houses over scattered in my yard—a nail, of all things, fell from the wood and sat there, unmoved and in perfect condition, all this time. There were twenty of them, all in a flawless row.

I thought about everyone and everything that did not get the same kind of treatment from the rushing water. But then I stopped myself, determined to slow my frantic thinking.

"He is near me," I said. "He will save my crushed spirit. I will not be broken."

And with that, I found the peace and resolve I needed to continue making my way down the fence line, hammering each nail back into the post it was pulled from, tightening the wire and restoring the fence.

I scrubbed each board in the barn and watched with a strange sense of comfort as the mud and leaves dripped off. I washed away the dingy coat that stood for what had happened in that place, revealing what looked like new wood beneath.

I unclipped the buckets, the only objects that remained in the building. They hung there unscathed, forcing me to remember what my normal used to be, the last reminders of the purpose this sad old structure once stood for. It felt just the same to unclip them now as when I did it twice a day for seven years. They sounded with the same click that made both horses delight in the arrival of dinner.

But now the click came and no nickers joined in. Instead, there was a click and then nothing, emptiness echoing through the stall wall, reminding me of the emptiness surrounding me.

Click.

I hit the ground and dropped my head. I was caving, despite the return of my confidence.

Then I reminded myself, "Near to the brokenhearted. Saves the crushed in spirit. I will not be broken."

I stood back up. Defeat had crept in on me, but I was unwilling to give it a home.

I tilted my head back and tried again. "He is near to my broken heart," I said. "He will save my crushed spirit. He will not let me be broken."

I let the tears come—they needed to—but I refused to let them halt my progress. I knew only the broken stopped moving.

Eventually I decided *clean* wasn't good enough for this barn. It had to be better.

I bought a beautiful brown wood stain and began working my way along each board. The stalls and the columns now gleamed in a grand new way. I made flower boxes and filled them with something of every color in the rainbow, forcing a bright light to shine in there, fighting back against the darkness.

I dragged a swing my father-in-law had made for us out of Brad's shop. It had sat in there, waiting to be hung, when the water rose. I scrubbed off the leaves and mud and then coated it with its own layer of the brown wood stain.

Then Brad hung it from the rafters of my beautiful, "like new" barn, the same rafters that had threatened to trap us months earlier. I stared up at those boards and remembered that chilling moment but found solace in the fact that its memory was no longer able to bring me to my knees.

The sun was dropping down in the sky, and orange flecks snuck through the pine trees in the front of our yard, indicating the end to another long but productive day. Ruth was in the living room watching an animated movie about a wild horse. It seemed like a good idea when I bought it for her, but I kicked myself when I noticed the plot had brought the horse to near drowning in a river.

"Who makes this stuff up for kids?" I muttered.

I didn't know if I should shut it off or let the story line play out, knowing most animated movies end well, give or take a dead parent or two. This was the second movie she'd watched in the past month that included near-drowning scenes for animals, and I was already scripting letters in my head to both production companies. I didn't want to play on the same old cliché, but, seriously, why not let them be little?

Ruth looked up and gazed at my face. How had I gotten such a sweet kid? How was she still putting up with me after the months we had been living? I never imagined, in my wildest dreams, I would be failing her so terribly at this point. I couldn't even pick out a movie that wasn't traumatic.

"It's okay, Mom," she said. "It's going to end okay."

That took the cake. She was stepping in as *my* rock now. *She* was comforting *me*. I needed to get myself together and up my parenting game before she ended up on a TLC reality show.

Then she said, "Mommy, I miss Jacky. Do you miss Gray-Gray?"

She told me she missed the horses constantly. At least once a day, we talked about the flood or Jack or Grady. I had hoped it would fade or that she would find peace, but she had the memory of an elephant and was well aware of her losses. She was still processing and was not yet okay.

I decided we were going to fill that void. We would be clear we weren't replacing Jack, but I was going to find her a new horse to love. A new mouth to feed. A new back to scratch. A new hero for her fairy tales.

For weeks, I scoured the Internet, searching for the perfect pony. Soon my determination was replaced with discouragement. Every single horse I found was either too expensive or located across the country.

Then one night, while I was sitting in bed, scrolling through horse ads, I found the sweetest looking buckskin paint I had ever seen.

"SHADOW," the ad said at the top. "Perfect kids' horse."

I studied the picture. She was impeccably built and stood quietly in the photograph, holding a little boy on her back and looking right at home with him.

She's probably in Nevada, I thought as I opened the ad.

Goose bumps ran down my arm when I saw she wasn't in Nevada or Oregon or even Alabama. She was in the next town over.

The next morning, I called the number on the ad and talked to the owner for a while. It turned out Shadow had made the news in the flood. There was footage of her being rescued from the water. *A little survivor*, I thought as I hung up the phone. *Just like us*.

A few days later, we turned into our driveway pulling our little white trailer with Shadow in the back. Ruth was over the moon as she fastened a brand-new pink halter to Shadow's pretty little head.

Even though she came into our lives in an effort to heal Ruth, I soon discovered Shadow seemed determined to love me. She followed me around and came the moment I called her. She sat still while I leaned my back against hers to contemplate the day. She wanted to be around me as much as I wanted to be around her. Maybe we were good for each other's souls.

"We made it, didn't we?" I asked her one evening. I had walked down to feed her and stood lingering in her company. It felt good to rub her soft muzzle and feel her breath in the palm of my hand. "We made it out."

She exhaled as I rested my head in her long white mane. Then she nuzzled me, exactly the way Jack used to do. My soul felt like it had found some small measure of rest in her presence.

"I'm so grateful for you, my sweet girl," I said, leaning into her and giving her one last good scratch before heading up for the night.

A cold and dreary November morning brought with it the news of my great-aunt's passing. Her witness had lived in my heart every day since her letter had arrived in my mailbox a few short months before. Now I was sitting in a pew at her church in Lexington, Virginia, saying goodbye to a woman who had changed my life with one small card. One gesture. One answered nudge.

Another nudge had brought Ruth and me here, to the church that was my great-aunt's home. I hadn't felt ready to come. Leaving town and traveling all that way terrified me. But I followed the lead of her obedience and trusted that God would protect my pets while we were gone.

I studied the words of a hymn inserted into the bulletin that had been given to me as I walked into the beautiful sanctuary. It was written about my aunt, in celebration of the work she did throughout her lifetime, ministering through music. The lyrics were artfully sculpted to represent her in song. They spoke of a fine-tuned vessel of the Lord, perfected through years of learning to listen and respond to God's will, "echoing the Sprit's music, through the witness of our deeds." What a perfect way to say it.

I watched as the hand-bell choir stood and celebrated her through delicate rings. I remembered listening to her sweet melodies as they rang through the grapevines that separated her home from ours on Martha's Vineyard. Some days she played a harp; on others, a grand piano. No matter the instrument, it was always beautiful. She was God's music. She was His vessel. Her witness was a gift, just like her many talents.

When the service ended, we followed the droves of people as they descended upon the auditorium to pay their respects to my cousins, who stood in a line, each of them a unique reflection of their two outstanding parents. I hugged them all and then went to study the photos and articles that were framed and presented atop a grand piano in the corner of the room.

I saw a picture of my great-aunt at a much younger age, taken when she had presumably just arrived in Lexington as a new mom, just starting her journey. I pictured the tiny island on which she had been raised and imagined her leaving it for college in New Hampshire, then going to Boston while her husband attended Harvard, then settling down in this new and unfamiliar place a few years later.

She had to have felt overwhelmed by it at times. She had come from such simple beginnings. Her father was a farmer on a then unknown island. He was a carpenter, a hardware store owner, and the superintendent of schools. He was a jack of all trades because he had to be for his little family to survive in such a humble place. It wasn't the Martha's Vineyard of the Kennedys at that point. It was a small town that ran on agriculture and hard work. But this new town, Lexington, where she had come to start her family, had two college campuses and masses of unknown people. It had to have felt so big to that small-town girl.

I thought of the church she had left behind on Martha's Vineyard, its beautiful stone exterior and perfect stained-glass walls. It stood high on a hill, overlooking Vineyard Haven Harbor, and was built by my great-grandfather, who was her father, after the first one burned down years before.

Surely she had longed for that church after she set out on her own. Surely she had missed the safety of that familiar congregation, full of family members and rich in heritage. Surely she had considered how much more comforting it could have been to have stayed home in that place with her people, rather than setting out to build an entirely new church family for herself here.

But staring at those pictures, the testaments of her life, I knew with all certainty that this was exactly what that young woman did. She set herself in motion, despite how daunting it may have been, and transformed her new community through her presence—a presence that hinged on her commitment to God's work. She found a new place to call home and committed her life to it. She immersed herself in that new congregation, and, judging by the faces of all these people, she had touched many lives in no small way.

When I headed home later that day, I knew I needed to follow her lead. I needed to step outside myself, overcome my fears, find a new church in the city where I lived, and commit myself to the people there. I needed to stop clinging to the memory of the place I had left behind.

It was a chilly day in December, not long after that, when I grabbed the mail and headed inside the house. I flipped through the toy catalogs and holiday mailers and then stopped at a glossy postcard sent by the church we had attended a few times after we had moved. We had told ourselves we would keep going back, but we'd gotten sidetracked by summer vacations and then halted by the flood.

I could hear the round of excuses playing in my mind. It was a little too far, or maybe a little too big. I'd always been great at excusing my way out of a bigger issue, and I could feel myself doing it again.

The truth was that this place had been on my mind a lot. They were a known force in our community for flood relief, which meant they didn't just quietly worship God with closed doors on Sunday mornings but showed our town what God's love looked like in action.

I flipped the postcard against my hand. It wasn't just an invitation to a Christmas service. It was an invitation to go home.

I read the line printed along the top:

> The people who walk in darkness
> will see a great light.
> For those who live in a land of deep darkness,
> a light will shine.
>
> —Isaiah 9:2

I loved those words. They were from the Old Testament prophecy of the birth of Jesus, the birth that promised a new kind of hope and a new kind of light more amazing than anything anyone before it could have imagined. A light that would deny all darkness.

I studied the list of Christmas services the church would hold. I looked at the lines of words and times, and all I could see or hear were the words "Go home."

I hung the glossy card on the fridge. I knew I needed this church in my life, and maybe Christmas, and its promise of new beginnings, was the perfect time to get myself there.

A few weeks later, I found myself standing on the curb of that massive stone church. Maybe it was the bustle of Christmas, or maybe it was the boxwood I noticed just off the sidewalk, but it felt like home.

I stepped over the threshold and took a seat inside the sanctuary. The children's service had a living nativity set up in front. Mary, Joseph, and a surprisingly well-behaved baby Jesus sat under a small makeshift manger in front of the congregation.

I thought back to the Christmases of my childhood. A family in our church would open their home and their stable every year for a living nativity. They set it up in a small outbuilding next to their barn. It was dimly lit, and straw and pine branches surrounded the perfectly silent holy family. I remember walking through it each year and getting chills at the wonder of it all. It relayed the true magic of Christmas to my little heart back then: a young family, tucked away in a tiny stall with livestock, doting over a newborn baby in a manger for a crib. They brought Christmas to life for us.

As my mind wandered, I caught a glimpse of a solitary brass cross sitting in front of the pulpit. All too often, I overlooked the cross, deeming it merely a symbol rather than an actual object upon which the greatest man to walk this earth died.

My eyes stayed glued to the cross. It stood in the foreground of that perfect nativity scene. The juxtaposition made me think how, every Christmas, I jumped at the opportunity to relive and experience the magic of the birth of Christ with living people in a living nativity scene. I wanted it to come alive. I wanted to feel close to the reality. But I would never wish that for the crucifixion. I didn't want to see that cross made of wood. I didn't want to see Jesus carry it up a hill in the hot afternoon sun. I didn't want to imagine His hands and feet nailed to it or to stand by and watch as He was mocked and harassed while He slowly suffocated.

I looked at the baby lying in the manger, tiny and perfect, and remembered the grown man kneeling in the garden, begging His Father to deliver Him from the fate He knew was coming for Him. Begging Him to take the cup. He was still God's Son, just taller and older. No less loved than the tiny baby being doted on in the manger. No less treasured.

I watched the eyes of the young mother portraying Mary. They were filled with an abundance of love for the little infant before her.

Then I imagined the real Mary, huddled helplessly at Jesus's feet while He was crucified. I imagined God watching His Son and hearing Him cry out in His final moments, asking why He had been forsaken.

I sat in that new pew, surveying the scene of joy at the birth of Jesus—a joy we relish, despite those three hours He spent dying on the cross. I wondered why I had never unleashed my colorful imagination on that other scene before. Had I been too young at first to process the magnitude of it? Too self-centered as a teen to fathom one human being tortured to death in order to save another? Did I choose to opt out of that too, as I had the questions related to suffering and how God leads? As an adult and a parent, did I gloss over it because the idea of kneeling at your child's feet while they were murdered was too much for a heart to handle?

Maybe I skipped over the crucifixion in the same way I failed to prioritize Good Friday services but always made it to church on Easter Sunday, my eyes fixed on the resurrection I knew was coming, the part where I would be made new by the sacrifice that was Jesus's suffering and dying. I just want to see the stone rolled away.

All too often, I spent Good Friday planning Easter

egg hunts, making grocery lists, and filling baskets with jelly beans and fake grass instead of letting my heart hang on that cross with Him. If I had done that sooner, maybe suffering would have made much more sense to me over the years.

I recalled what Jesus said:

> "I tell you the truth, you will weep and mourn over what is going to happen to me, but the world will rejoice. You will grieve, but your grief will suddenly turn to wonderful joy. It will be like a woman suffering the pains of labor. When her child is born, her anguish gives way to joy because she has brought a new baby into the world."
>
> —JOHN 16:20–21

As I studied the cross, I realized the answer to the anguish of suffering wasn't found in figuring out why it happened. Maybe, instead, it was in seeing that it gives way to great joy. The tiny baby in the manger did die on the cross, and it was terrible and horrible and I was sure it was hard to make sense of on that day. But the story didn't end there. The story, as the postcard from a few weeks earlier reminded me, ended in great light being cast over great darkness, a light that promised hope in tragedy.

On the drive home, I played with words in my head. *Resurrection* and *restoration*—the words were synonymous. They revive things. In the same way God knew Jesus had to die on the cross, He also knew that sometimes our greatest tragedies can bring us new life. He could have saved Jesus, and He could have stepped in and given me a miracle in the middle of the flood. But He knew Jesus would save the world through the resurrection. Maybe He wanted to see me roll a stone of my own away.

When we turned down our road, I felt a renewed sense of hope. We passed vacant houses with temporary trailers parked in front of them. Wreaths hung on their doors. White lights sparkled off fences that had lain on their sides a few months earlier.

We rounded the bend and passed my old neighbor's beautiful home. The Dumpster still blocked the driveway. The rug still hung from the railing. But now a life-sized sign stood in the front yard, proclaiming one word: JOY.

I glimpsed a few stocky quarter horses grazing off in the distance. The sun sparkled on their shiny backs.

"Little survivors," I whispered under my breath with a smile.

Chapter 8

IT WAS THE first day of a new year and I was sitting in my new pew in the new church in the heart of downtown Baton Rouge. I was grappling with God over its size. Why not nudge me toward something smaller, less intimidating?

Still, a nudge was a nudge, and I was trying to be in the business of obedience and trust.

So there I sat, optimistic that somehow, in this large church, I would find a way to feel at home, even though when I walked up the long line of stone stairs and crossed the threshold, taking in row after row of people, I had a hard time believing that could happen.

I flipped through the bulletin during the opening announcements. An inserted sheet portrayed a picture of a group of women. It was an invitation for a ministry the church had for mothers. It used the word *small* in the description, and I liked small. It had the word *mom* in the name, and I was a mom.

I looked at the picture and imagined the steps I would have to take to get there. They were steps toward a new group of women, and women, especially in groups, terrified me. Women could be mean. Historically, women didn't get me. A group of women was the opposite of the cave that on some days I still thought would be the best option for me.

Then came the nudge.

Why couldn't God be satisfied with my making it to church two weeks in a row and leave me alone for a minute? What ever happened to baby steps? This little sheet of paper, joining this women's group, was not a baby step. It was a leap.

I studied the picture. Would they like me? Would they judge me? Would they size up my parenting choices and pick apart my appearance? Would they want to know where my husband worked and care about what kind of car I drove? Or, worse, would they look inside my car and find the two pairs of flip-flops, the empty bag of popcorn, the twelve Barbies, and the coffee cup from three days ago?

Then what?

I tucked the sheet into my purse and decided I would think about it—and hope God changed His mind.

The following week, I was standing in my garden, pulling weeds and working through my prayers, and couldn't stop thinking about that group at church. I had missed the first week of their gathering because I was still unsure if I could bring myself to go. I was wrestling with God on it, and He was winning. Every time I said no, an image of me scanning the church and wondering if it would ever feel like home popped into my head.

I was scared. But something in me knew that if God wanted me there, it had to be a safe place for me.

I rubbed my dirt-soiled hands on my tattered pair of jeans and grabbed my phone. I called the number on the ad and was connected by the operator to the welcoming director at the church. She sounded kind. She was a member of the mom group and offered to meet me in the parking lot for the next meeting and walk in with me.

How did she know I had issues with thresholds?

The following morning, I gathered up Ruth and my things to go to the meeting and glanced at the photograph of my grandfather, which was now on my wall. I looked at his face and wondered if anyone I would meet that day would fill my heart with joy in the same way his Saturday Morning Saints group had filled his. Would I find people with whom I could "walk in the light of His Word"?

I pulled out of the driveway, and a reel of questions ran through my mind. Would they embrace a new member? Did they even want a new member?

I scrolled through the mental checklist of areas where I always seemed to strike out. When I didn't say enough, people thought I was an expletive that starts with a B. When I spoke too much, I was thought to be too assertive. When I was completely and most truly myself, I was discounted as disingenuous.

I knew these things. They had been passed down to me over the years. I never hit homeruns in the first-impression department. I was more of a fourth- or fifth-impression girl.

Would they size up my background? My lack of a career? Would they wonder why I hadn't attended church regularly the last ten years?

With every question came a silent assurance that this was the church where I needed to be and this was a group God wanted me to join. I wasn't going alone. He was going with me.

When I pulled into the parking lot of the church and unbuckled Ruth from her car seat, I was nervous, but the welcoming director met me at the door, as she promised. I studied her face. I didn't sense anything fake or contrived about her. Sure, it was her job to welcome people, but her heart seemed in it too.

We walked through the maze of the church, dropping Ruth off in the nursery, and then headed to a separate building, where our group would meet.

When I stepped over the threshold and into that room, I wasn't met with judgment or criticism. I didn't find a collection of complex people who said one thing but thought another. I wasn't picked apart or excluded. Instead, I found a group of smart, hilarious, and kind women. I sensed they too were committed to trust and obedience and were intent on seeking with their whole hearts.

Later that week, I stood in my kitchen, finishing my coffee, and looked outside. It looked cold, so I pulled a heavy jacket onto Ruth's body and kissed her nose.

"It's time to go feed Shadow Girl," I said with a smile.

Her eyes widened, and she ran to the back door and twisted it open with her knit-mittened hand.

We walked down to the barn, and Shadow met us at the back of her pasture. Ruth ran ahead of me, and I smiled, watching them together. Shadow leaned her head down to Ruth's level and blew soft breaths down on her mess of blonde hair. The horse had an air of peace about her and a knack for loving little girls.

When we got to the barn, I rummaged in the bright red feed cart that had recently made its way back into our lives. My neighbor had found it suspended in some trees on his two-hundred-acre hunting property. It was just a big plastic box with wheels, but it felt good to get something back from the woods.

I pulled back, looking at the cart, and laughed, remembering the lifetime warranty that came with its purchase. The sellers purported it could withstand all wear and tear. I wondered if they knew it could come back from five months spent in a pine tree after a flood. Maybe I should write them a letter.

I heard a loud bang in the distance, and Shadow's eyes shot up with concern. It was hunting season, and being surrounded by woods meant hearing the occasional loud bang.

But bang or no bang, it seemed our sweet horse was getting less relaxed lately, and I wondered if maybe her solitude had something to do with it. I had never intended to keep her alone forever, though initially she seemed to like it. Horses are herd animals. They get their strength and comfort in numbers. As laid back as our sweet girl was, when things got tense, she needed a friend. I understood that.

I stared at the vacant stall and felt the heavy pit of grief that still sat in my soul whenever I peeked inside it. I knew it wasn't grief alone that weighed on me. It was guilt. And that guilt was the most stubborn of emotions. Getting Ruth a new horse had been easy. I wanted to lift her up. I wanted to brighten her world. I wanted to fill the void in her little life and give her someone new to bring her joy.

Filling the second spot in our stable was more complicated. I didn't know if I deserved to have that void filled. Maybe I had earned that empty stall and the hole in my heart that accompanied it.

Later that afternoon, I put Ruth down for her nap and stepped outside. I walked to the garden and grabbed the tiny olive tree that had been sitting there, unplanted, since I purchased it a few weeks before. Then I headed, tree in hand, down the dirt road to where Jack and Grady now lie together, high on the hill I had hoped would provide them safety from any flood.

I crossed the quiet creek. I passed the line of fence and studied each board that was now standing upright, repaired. I walked by the barn and ran my fingers along its weathered sides. I glanced up at the branches I had left hanging high in the rafters as a reminder of that night.

As I climbed the hill, I noticed the sun peeking out from between the trees. Its rays beamed down on the two giant stones my brother had brought from my favorite beach to mark the horses' place. I stopped at the top of the hill and looked down on their graves. I knew they were down there, somewhere beneath my feet. In my heart, but no longer within my reach.

I wanted nothing more from my relationship with those two animals than to keep them free from harm. There weren't any other absolutes between us. I didn't care if they performed well or if we soared to any great heights in a competition. My only goal was for them to be happy, cared for, and safe.

Why didn't I think the rain that day was a threat to those three things? Why hadn't I seen it as deadly? Why had I been so utterly confident in numbers and charts and river forecasts? Why did I place so much faith in what had happened in March and in the information of strangers?

I stared at the ground.

It was because I'm imperfect. And I would be, regardless of the events of August 12, 2016. I'm an imperfect person living an imperfect life, making imperfect decisions in an imperfect world. And that is okay. That's what being a human is about.

God knew that, even when I did not. It's why He wanted me to stop leading and follow. Somewhere down the line, I got so tangled up in myself that I forgot to recognize my humanness. I thought I could rely on my instincts and my decision-making skills alone. I had put the weight of the world on my two shoulders—shoulders that were never intended to bear such a heavy load.

Maybe instead of finding strength in my abilities, I needed to focus on finding strength and comfort in my God-given size. I have a Father in heaven who *is* built for the weight of the world.

I crouched down and dug up the soil, filling part of their grave with the fresh, young roots of the tiny olive tree. As I tamped the ground lightly, I leaned forward and whispered to them one last time, "I am so, so sorry, my sweet boys."

I was the only one who needed to hear it.

I stood up and tilted my head back. A mass of magnolia trees towered high above my head. Giant oaks seemed to wrap around me. I breathed in the solitude and then looked down at the freshly stirred soil at my feet.

This would no longer be a place I came to drown my soul in the mistakes of my past. It was where I would come to be reminded of my call to humility and the gift God had given me in His limitless mercy and grace. He already knew I couldn't do anything on my own. I was the only one who needed to learn that.

Throughout my life, I had ridden horses with limitations—horses who were skittish, unpredictable, poorly trained, or physically restricted. I'd always felt lucky to ride, so I never cared much either way. But I often wondered what it would be like to have a horse with an abundance of potential, one who would only be limited as far as I placed the limits.

Grady had been that horse. He was young, and his only drawback was his age and lack of experience. He was a magnificent blank slate with strong fundamentals and impeccable breeding.

I have a picture of Grady from a horse show the year before Ruth was born. It was raining, and being wet made his jet-black coat look even more majestic. He was soaring over a jump and doing so in such a stylish way that it made me look far more accomplished than I actually was in a saddle. It was a great shot, but it wasn't my favorite.

My favorite picture of Grady was taken about

three months before he died. I was working on the tractor in his pasture, and he had placed his whole head in the big orange bucket of the front-end loader, trying to see what was inside of it and making it impossible for me to do anything other than take his picture. He was a practical joker. My class clown. A big, beautiful personality that craved human contact.

That was the pet I missed.

I missed him making me laugh and disrupting my progress. I missed his quirky companionship.

I didn't care if I ever set foot in another arena again as long as I lived. I didn't care if I never got to feel the power of a horse taking flight from beneath me again. It was all wonderful and amazing, and I was grateful I was able to participate in that sport, but it was not what drove me to own horses. I loved the company of horses. I loved their personalities. I loved how silly some of them were. They were good for my soul.

If I was going to find a new pet to fill Grady's stall, then that animal had to be, above all things, hilarious.

Days later, I found myself back to trolling horse ads. Once again, I was frustrated by geography. I wasn't about to commit to eight hours on the road. I couldn't, especially when horse shopping could turn up a lot of dead ends. I needed to find a horse Ruth and I could visit together.

Then one afternoon, I found a picture of an almost-red quarter horse with a white face and two huge blue eyes. I laughed out loud. He was both ridiculous and beautiful. I read his description. *Easy to ride. Loves to be brushed.* Then the best part: He was located in the next town over.

A few days later, I led him into his new home and latched the door behind him. He was fun to ride, but he also gave the distinct impression of being fun to love.

We renamed him Mesquite because he was the same color as the inside of those trees.

After I locked his door that first night, I looked at the scene around me. Shadow and Mesquite quietly munching hay. The barn restored. The things we needed tucked into new trunks and stored away.

I studied them both and then looked up at the branches in the rafters, knowing I would never respond to excessive rain in a casual way again. But I also understood disasters come in all sorts of packages outside of my control. It was not up to me to try to imagine every possible scenario. It was not up to me to worry and lament outcomes that may never come to fruition. I needed to be smart and make good, safe decisions, but that was where my responsibility ended and Someone more powerful and capable took over.

It was a blustery January morning, and the sky was dark as the rain pounded our roof. It was pouring onto the porch outside our bedroom window, and I shivered at the reminder of the flood and the feeling that the rain wouldn't stop until it consumed us. The darkness overshadowed what should have been daylight, and the whole scene made me feel weak and defenseless.

"I miss the days when I loved the rain," I said to Brad as I stood watching the overflowing pond.

He was getting ready for work, and he walked over to me and rubbed my back.

The forecast called for heavy rain and the potential for strong storms. We hadn't had much precipitation since the flood, and I'd been happier that way. I didn't trust weather anymore.

I stepped back from the window and walked to the kitchen to make Ruth's lunch for school. I pulled out her bright pink owl lunchbox and set to work filling it with a sandwich, sliced grapes, and a bag of crackers.

I heard the rumble of thunder in the distance, and my arms tensed like they do when my body would prefer I stop moving and find a cave.

Ruth woke up, and I went through the motions of getting her ready for school, pulling a fresh new pair of pants on her legs, sliding a soft, warm shirt over her little arms, tying shoes onto her sweet feet. Each bolt of lightning and crash of thunder encouraged me to retreat and call her in sick that day, keeping her safely within my reach. I could still remember that morning after the flood, gripping tightly to her life preserver and not letting her out of my sight.

I couldn't find the middle of the road within myself anymore. I couldn't determine the difference between cautious and overbearing.

Before the flood, I had been fairly optimistic about outcomes. I encouraged Ruth to be independent and to explore the world within the confines of what I found reasonable for someone her age. I wanted her to wander. I wanted her to explore. I wanted her to build the confidence that comes from all of that. I would stand in the horses' stalls, silently grooming them while listening to her set off with our dogs into the wild, wondrous world of our backyard.

In the days since the flood, I had leashed that side of her. I held tight to that leash, knowing I needed to release it, but I wasn't sure how.

I loaded Ruth into the car and set off down the road, gripping my steering wheel with knuckles that were nearly white. The rain poured down in sheets around me, and goose bumps formed on the surface of my skin. I couldn't do this. The sights and sounds were too familiar. They looked too much like the day my world had changed.

I looked in my rearview mirror and thought about

Ruth. Somewhere along the way, she had relented to the fear alongside me. Somewhere between the flood and the changes it had evoked in me, she had been defeated herself. She was also convinced the world was a dangerous place.

I knew if I turned the car around and retreated to the comfort of our home, those actions would confirm that for her. It would confirm it for both of us.

I pulled up at a stoplight in the center of town, grateful for the opportunity to take a break from trying to see the road. I focused on the three lights before me, then snuck a peek in my rearview mirror. My sweet girl sat staring out of her window with a grimace plastered on her delicate face.

"Are you excited for school?" I hollered over the rain, trying to distract her mind from the place I knew it was going.

Her gaze was locked on the water pooling on the lawn of a home that was set back from the road. "Is it going to flood again?" she replied.

I rested my head against the seat and rubbed my temples with a sigh. I really didn't know how to respond to that. Chances were that we would never get that kind of rain again in either of our lifetimes. But chances had failed us once before. These days, every single cloud that formed in the sky seemed capable of delivering a fatal blow. Each drop of rain seemed destined to knock us off of the weak foundation we had only recently dragged ourselves onto. Security seemed like a distant hope, as silly as yearning for Christmas in the middle of January.

I used to find a whole lot of comfort in numbers. I liked knowing the likelihood of any given outcome. I loved to weigh odds. I clung to low percentages when I was afraid of something, like a shark attack, a plane crash, deadly illnesses, or snake bites. I liked knowing a number out there could indicate such a thing was rare.

But the flood taught me that rare and impossible are two completely different things. Rare is unlikely but still possible. Someone out there *is* going to be attacked by a shark. People *will* die in plane crashes. Strange and mysterious illnesses *could* afflict some people, even children. Odd accidents *do* happen. Tornados *can* wipe out entire towns. And thousand-year rains *will* fall and cause thousand-year floods. Because while all these things are rare, they are still possible.

Numbers had failed me, and now my system was broken. The world felt like a dangerous place, with tragedy always lurking, the threat of every rare thing that now felt quite possible.

I didn't know how to answer Ruth. I wanted the answer myself.

I turned the music on and tried to distract her with Taylor Swift, but the song was interrupted by the emergency alert system instructing people in our area to take shelter immediately. A tornado had formed in the next town over—the same tiny town where Ruth's school was located.

I was driving toward a tornado.

I looked down the road. About three miles stood between us and her school. At least fifteen stood between us and our house. I felt trapped. I had no idea which way to go.

The sky was black, and the clouds blanketed the space just above us. Thunder rumbled in the distance, and lightning lit up the sky in rapid succession.

I wanted to shut down, but I couldn't. My baby was strapped into the back seat.

I finished the drive to school, feeling like I should run away but unsure which direction made sense. We got to the parking lot, and the teachers at the school rushed us inside. All of the children, teachers, and a few parents were sitting in a line along the interior hallway of the building. I looked up and down the aisle at the faces of the kids, many of whom had lost their homes in the flood only a few months before. To make it worse, most flood victims were residing in government-issued mobile homes and campers, some of the least secure places to be when a tornado hits.

The weight of it was heavy. Heavier than I could bear.

I watched the kids playing in the hallway, unaware of the danger swirling above us, the new threat that added to the adults' collective mood of unease.

I knew I wasn't supposed to be afraid, but how

could I not be? I sat with my back against the brick wall and scrolled through a googled list of scriptures about fear and courage. Eventually I settled on this one:

> "Have I not commanded you? Be strong and courageous. Do not be afraid; do not be discouraged, for the LORD your God will be with you wherever you go."
>
> —JOSHUA 1:9, NIV

I read the words over and over again, occasionally glancing out the glass doors at the black sky above us. I believed the words. I didn't doubt them. But how did I do it?

Eventually the clouds lifted over the school, and the tornado warning ended. I kissed Ruth goodbye and headed out to my car, which I'd parked haphazardly in the drenched parking lot an hour before. I remembered us running through the pouring rain. I was sick of running from stuff. I was sick of running away.

I got home and watched as new black clouds filled the sky and my phone lit up with a new tornado warning. A new call to take shelter. I closed the warning and flipped to the screenshot I had taken of Joshua 1:9. *He was with me wherever I went.*

I sat and watched the clouds and wished fifteen miles didn't separate Ruth and me. I wished we had stayed home. I wasn't ready to battle weather. I wanted to shelter in place with her by my side, just as we had that first morning after the flood. I wanted to be a life preserver. I wanted a body big enough to shield her from a tornado. I wanted to be her cave.

But God was telling me to be courageous instead. Courageous people don't hang out in caves.

I reached for my Bible and started thumbing through it. I needed an example. I needed someone other than Joshua. I was not a Joshua. Joshua was a bold and courageous leader; I was a scared, middle-aged girl. I needed a hero I could relate to.

I flipped farther, past David slaying Goliath. Past the story of Elijah being beckoned from the comfort of his own cave by God's whisper. Past Zerubbabel leading the exiles back from Babylon. I was none of those people. I couldn't find myself in any of those shining examples of great faith.

My fingers stopped flipping on the first page of the book of Esther. The story of the orphaned Jewish girl who lived in the palace of the king of Persia as his queen, her roots hidden.

Esther, I could relate to. Esther had not made it home yet. Esther was someone who had spent her whole life denying God and then had to call on Him for help when she was in a bind.

I read the text of the story again, for the first time in ages, and pictured her. Her distance from God was implied in each detail: a member of the exiled tribe of Benjamin who chose to remain in a pagan land and assimilated so much that no one, not even her husband, knew she was a Jew.

I could feel Esther in me. She had wandered far from home, and up until that point nothing bad enough had happened to convince her to turn around and run back. She hovered between dueling identities.

Then her world got shaken. The king issued an edict for the destruction of her people: "All Jews—young and old, including women and children—must be killed, slaughtered, and annihilated on a single day" (Esther 3:13).

Yikes. I sat back after reading those words and pictured a message like that showing up on my doorstep. I watched the rain pour down outside and studied the black clouds cast before me. I pictured the children at Ruth's school running around in the halls and then imagined all of the Jewish boys and girls running through the streets of Susa on the day this message was delivered to their parents.

They didn't have many options, but they did have one of their own people tucked away in the palace. Esther's cousin, Mordecai, sent a message to her and asked her to be brave and go to the king to "beg for mercy and plead for her people" (Esther 4:8).

With that verse, it seemed simple. Of course she should go to her husband and save them all. Of course she would. Problem solved. Jews saved.

But as I read on, I realized the Persian Empire, in which Esther lived, did not look anything like the twenty-first-century America I knew. This was no "text your husband to pick up Chinese food" scenario.

There was nothing simple about this for her. It was complicated, messy, and scary.

Esther's husband was the king of Persia, the most powerful empire in the world at that time. She did not have an open line of communication with him. He hadn't even "called" for her in thirty days. I wasn't there, but in reading the story, I didn't get the impression the two of them were riding on a wave of marital bliss, arm in arm. Chasing butterflies. Picking wildflowers.

In chapter 1 of the book, before Esther comes on the scene, the king banished his first wife, Vashti, for disrespecting him at a party. The book of Esther does not paint the picture of a husband who wants to carry out the wishes of his wife. He doesn't seem approachable or predictable. Instead, he seems like an often drunk, easily misled, hot-headed party boy. What's worse is that, by law, Esther could be put to death simply for approaching the king without being invited to do so.

Esther didn't want to approach the king. She didn't want to ask him for anything. She didn't want to expose herself in any way, shape, or form. It sounded to me like Esther wanted a cave. She wanted to ride the tide of being safe in the king's palace. She wanted to stay under his radar and self-preserve.

I got Esther. I loved to self-preserve.

But then Mordecai dug deep with his next message:

> "Don't think that for a moment that because you're in the palace you will escape when all the other Jews are killed. If you keep quiet at a time like this, deliverance and relief for the Jews will arise from some other place, but you and your relatives will die. Who knows if perhaps you were made queen for just such a time as this?"
>
> —Esther 4:13–14

That was heavy to read.

I sat back on thc couch and thought about that moment. I pictured Esther wanting to shelter herself and Mordecai pointing out how flimsy the idea of shelter really was.

My phone dinged with a new tornado warning. Lightning flashed just past the pond. My arms tensed as I checked the clock to see how much time I had left before I could pick up Ruth.

I wondered if Esther's body locked at the thought of approaching the king.

I bent my arm back and forth a few times and wondered if her limbs flowed freely in the face of her danger. Did she move with ease? She had to have felt terrified. Like me the morning after the flood, trying to choose between the house and the boat, no option feeling comfortable enough. Then I remembered the severe weather booming on all sides of me right then, the drive to school, trying to race the clouds, knowing such an attempt was futile.

God's name isn't mentioned once in the pages of

Esther's story. Was He absent in her heart, as well? Did the distance that lay between them, after all of those years of wandering, affect her ability to find courage in the face of this grave danger? She was no Joshua, no Zerubbabel, no Elijah, and no David. She wasn't in a close relationship with God. She'd not spent her lifetime fine-tuning her ability to trust in Him. She'd spent a lifetime distancing herself from Him.

I wondered if she could picture her own sea parting before her. Could she visualize the mountain moving through blind faith in a God she had essentially disowned? Or did she struggle with it, as I did?

I read on and watched Esther find some courage—courage to move toward a fate that seemed certain of destruction. The law of her land stated that those who approached the king without being invited were "doomed to die."

Esther wasn't just afraid of a tornado. She walked into one, knowing it could very well be the end of her. She said:

> "Go and gather together all the Jews of Susa and fast for me. Do not eat or drink for three days, night or day. My maids and I will do the same. And then, though it is against the law, I will go in to see the king. If I must die, I must die."
>
> —Esther 4:16

All of a sudden, Esther was back to being a Jew. She was back inside her roots, where fasting was used as a mechanism to find God's direction. I can't tell as an outside and uneducated observer, but maybe this was the first time she ever sought God. She was young and living among an assimilated tribe in a pagan area. But she knew, deep down, what those roots believed, and she got down to the business of seeking with all of her heart.

In the chapters that followed, she devised a solid plan for winning the king's favor and saving the Jews. I wondered, Did she find that plan in the depths of her fast? In the depths of that silence? Did she find a new voice to guide her? A nudge she had not experienced before?

I rested my head on the back of the couch and imagined God. We, as people, have changed. Times have changed. But God has not. I wondered, staring at the page, if the same comfort I believed Esther found in her three-day fast, the comfort that enabled her to suit up and approach the king, was what I could find if I stayed focused on the knowledge that God is with me wherever I go.

Her last sentence replayed in my mind: "If I must die, I must die." Was part of the big picture the understanding that we have to let outcomes fly? To believe that God will protect us, whether in life or in death?

I closed my Bible, thankful for Esther, and grabbed my keys to go and pick up Ruth. Twenty minutes later, I parked at her school and watched as the kids poured out of the front door of the small brick building. None of their little souls seemed to carry the weight of that morning. They were happy, blissful children, armed with optimism for the afternoon ahead.

I paused and remembered myself at that age. My main problem in those years was a pair of monsters who frequented the closet just beyond my bed. I would wake up in the middle of the night frantic, certain they were advancing on me, as monsters sometimes do. My parents would rush in and make sure there were no monsters. My dad would tell me stories to clear my mind. Then they would say my prayers with me again and remind me that God always watched over me, even as the whole world slept.

After they left, I would lie in bed, staring at the ceiling, trying to picture how big God was. I imagined Him up there in the sky, staying awake all night to watch over me and all of the other little children everywhere.

That's big.

It didn't ever cross my mind that God wasn't capable of having His eyes on every person in the world at the same time. Kids don't question amazing feats as adults do. They believe so purely, and then they revel in the wonder of it. They haven't reached that point in their lives where they have to doubt things they can't fully comprehend. Kids have the capacity to see God for how big He really is. They can sing the words "He's got the whole world in His hands" and picture hands that are big enough to do that. They can close their eyes and know there's a spot somewhere in those hands just for them.

I was the one who still needed convincing that a wandering girl who picked her own path and abandoned God for a while still had a safe and secure spot in His hands. I was the one who needed to remind herself what the comfort of that spot felt like after all those years. I was the one who had to harness her inner Esther and remind herself that wherever she was, whether on a boat, on a plane, in a tornado, or in a palace in Persia, God was there and looking out for His people.

Two months later, the sun shone down on a beautiful spring morning, and I was taking Shadow and Mesquite to a friend's house so she could watch them while I traveled home to Boston for the first time in nearly a year. Prior to the flood, I had worn out the skies between the East Coast and my home in Baton Rouge, but travel was one of the areas that continued to paralyze me. I couldn't get past the worry that another rainy day would come and turn into another catastrophic flood while I was halfway across the country. Who would save my pets?

I knew, at that point, numbers couldn't protect me. I knew that every day, there was a .01 percent chance we would experience that exact kind of flood again. I knew that, as unlikely as it was, it could still happen.

As I healed and learned to lean on the Lord, I realized I needed to let go of this one. I needed to go home and see the people I loved back in Boston. I couldn't allow the fear that had grown inside me for all those months to continue to limit my motion. I needed to be strong and courageous and trust my outcomes to God.

I drove down the road that morning filled with confidence. I wasn't worried or apprehensive. The fear that had dominated my soul for eight months seemed to be quite in check.

After about ten miles, an error message came up on the screen of my truck, indicating a wiring fault. I checked the brakes and had no trouble, so I wondered if something was wrong with my lights. Coincidentally, some friends of ours who had been visiting for the weekend were driving down the road behind me. I called them on my phone and asked if my brake lights worked when I tapped them. They confirmed the lights were fine, and we hung up.

A few minutes later, they called back to tell me to pull over right away. Smoke was issuing from underneath the trailer.

Thankfully, I was a few feet from a gas station and pulled in. Now smoke billowed from the hub of my rear tires. Lots and lots of smoke. The trailer had nearly caught fire with my horses inside it.

Within seconds, all the fear I had worked so hard

to hand over to God came rushing back like a tidal wave. My body locked up, and I had to force my limbs to work. I was caught between complete shock at what had almost transpired and intense worry about what I was supposed to do next.

In which direction should I move? Was there a cave nearby with space enough for two equines? What was the safest next step?

All of the grief of the wrong decisions I had made in the flood took hold again. Do I unload both horses, right there on the side of the road? The road was dangerous in its own right. And if I did, where would I go from there? Was the trailer going to spontaneously combust?

I had to make the perfect decision with no knowledge of locked brakes or anything else of that nature. I knew how to drive a horse trailer, but I didn't know the mechanics of them. What was safe?

It was as if I was back at that Friday, weighing the decision to leave Jack and Grady high on a hill I was positive would not flood or bring them up by the road to stand out in the rain all night. I had tried to be a flood expert, and I had failed. I had tried to weigh the risks, and I had failed.

I called Brad and handed the phone to our friend, who was inspecting the undercarriage of the trailer. He tested the bearings, checked the brakes, ruled some other stuff out, and, with Brad's help, determined that the wires connecting the brakes to the truck had corroded and caused the brakes to lock. He unplugged the wire and resolved the issue.

I trusted Brad's and our friend's opinion. I knew if they told me something was safe, then it was. I knew staying in the parking lot for the rest of my life wasn't an option. I needed to move in one direction or another.

I got back into the truck and gripped my steering wheel. I felt like I was a cloud that had floated away from the place where I had only recently anchored myself—the place where I had promised to trust in God through any storm.

My favorite words from Zechariah came back to me: "Return to me, and I will return to you" (Zechariah 1:3). At that moment I felt like God was using those words to remind me to return to Him in my mind, regardless of what the terrain looked like before me or whether dark and ominous clouds had begun to form, threatening to bear down on my soul. God wanted to be with me in my storms.

I had improved in my daily walk with Him—the strolls through sunny and uneventful moments—but at the first sign of trouble, I regressed. I floated off and joined the storm clouds of fear that formed above me.

But what if I just tried… to return to Him?

I pictured God sitting in the truck beside me, gently prompting me to let Him lead the way out. I visualized Him plucking me out of the sky, straight out of the clouds, and setting me back down next to Him before I drifted off with my fears.

I returned to Him, and He returned to me.

I finished my drive and repeated those words the whole way. A wave of confidence filled me, and with it came the understanding that I was not alone and that I was safe. I was responsible for setting myself into motion. I was accountable for not making reckless decisions. But I was not in charge of outcomes. No one is.

I needed to force myself to move and act, even when I wanted to shut down, because that is what walking in faith is all about. I needed to follow Esther's lead on that. Faith is trusting the outcomes to God, not to the choices I make.

My mind ran through the events of the morning. Our friends had been staying with us from out of town. They happened to pull out of my driveway the same time I did, even though I'd encouraged them to stay behind as long as they wanted. I had pulled out in front of them, when they could have just as easily pulled out first. They happened to notice the smoke and called me just in time. There are many stretches of my road that have no place to pull over. Several parts are miles long and bendy, with deep ditches along the side. Gravel trucks fly down the road all day, making stopping inadvisable and potentially deadly. But a gas station was right in front of me when they called.

Terrible things could have happened that morning,

but they didn't. Instead, the journey was peppered with small but substantial miracles around every curve.

Chapter 9

THE SUN PEEKED out from behind the clouds on a mild Sunday morning as I pulled my car out of the driveway and headed toward church. We were going to be late, and frustration was boiling up to the surface in my already almost full pot. No sooner had I accelerated to my "running late" speed but a truck pulled in front of me, cutting me off and then slowing down to fifteen miles per hour slower than I wanted to be driving.

I barked an expletive at the stranger and slapped my steering wheel.

"What's that?" Ruth asked from the back seat, repeating the word I'd just said.

I cursed again, this time under my breath.

I rubbed my forehead. I was not winning any parenting prizes in that moment. I tried to find words to explain to my daughter why I had chosen to verbally assault a complete stranger behind his back on the way to church, but there aren't really any great words for that.

As the pointless explanation flowed from the well-oiled excuse-generating machine of my mind, I kicked myself for getting to the point where I was acting this way. I wasn't usually an angry person. I tended to expend most of my energy on worry, and there wasn't typically enough time or space in my brain for both.

Plus, not much produces anger in me. Or maybe not much used to. The flood had changed that. Anger simmered inside me constantly now. It had made itself at home in my soul.

I could still see that handwritten list of bullet points I'd written in my notebook just a few weeks after the flood. Anger was the last thing on the list of things I needed help with—the mountain I needed moved. But progress on this one was slow. Much slower than the rest. My anger was stubborn.

It had all started the night after the flood. I had gotten it into my mind that maybe, just maybe, Jack and Grady were still out there. And if, by some miracle, they were, they would need me. They could be hurt or scared or in the wrong hands.

So on that night, while fear gripped me and water still surrounded my house, I had posted a picture of them on the "lost pets" site for our town. I uploaded the picture, listing their last known location. I knew the outlook was bleak, but I still held hope in my heart.

I don't know what I expected would come from that effort, but I do know I did not expect a stranger to tell me she wouldn't have let that happen to her horse—that she would have died in order to save it.

I didn't expect that kind of treatment on that day. I wasn't prepared for it. I was already a disaster. Her comments weren't productive or helpful or kind. They were callous.

My reaction to that comment started out as hurt but morphed into anger.

Then, with each new day, more things added to that pot. There were the news articles that said Louisiana shouldn't be inhabited, that it was our fault we flooded and we shouldn't live here. They compared us to New Orleans, not realizing we are one hundred miles north of there in an area not prone to flooding—hence, the reason we were caught off guard by it.

People attacked pet owners who hadn't claimed their animals, unaware of the bind some people were in because they no longer had homes or cars or phones or even food for their own mouths, much less for a pet. Then there was the criticism of people whose pets were stuck in flooded homes.

Sometimes it takes seeing hundreds of abandoned cars lining major throughways, flooded and with broken windshields, to understand some people did not make it home. Some people couldn't *get* home. It was heartbreaking enough. No one needed to be kicked in the gut for it.

So on that morning, on our way to church, I was stewing in it all. Every new thing that happened, no matter how small, built on the existing pile, fueling my general assumption that some people can be—well, my outburst said it all.

Then I showed up at church and scanned the bulletin. My eyes widened, and I almost jumped out of my seat when I saw the title of the sermon that day: "The Danger of Anger."

Yikes. I was being called out… or followed.

I sat in my seat, eating up every word, knowing they were, in part, for me. Our pastor presented anger as more of a disease than a state of being, a condition we have to push against and something we are responsible for conquering. She made me realize my anger wasn't something I should wait to have clear up on its own, like a cold or a rash. It needed tending. This "issue within my spirit," as she put it, wasn't going to fix itself. I needed to put work into fixing it.

I looked at the Scripture reading for the day and drew a block around it with my pen. James 4.

Later that evening, I picked up my Bible and read the whole book of James. When I was done, I understood the big picture.

James's message centers on the idea of setting yourself aside in the interest of doing what we're expected to do as followers of Jesus. Jesus spent His time on earth showing us how to love. He reserved His anger for those whose behavior was shaped by obedience to laws and rituals and not driven by a changed spirit. He directed sharp words toward those who refused to allow the kind of transformation within themselves that would usher in a greater capacity for that all-encompassing love He wants us to extend to others. He didn't want lip service. He wanted changed hearts.

My eyes lingered on James 3:17, and I reached for my highlighter:

> But the wisdom from above is first of all pure. It is also peace loving, gentle at all times, and willing to yield to others. It is full of mercy and the fruit of good deeds. It shows no favoritism and is always sincere.

"Yield to others." Those words jumped into my soul. James was speaking my language. Yielding, or rather the refusal to yield, is a pet peeve of mine. It frustrates me when other drivers fail to yield. If I'm being honest, I make strong assumptions about the character of someone who disrupts the flow of traffic in that way. It grinds my gears. Road rage gets shut down if one driver is willing to switch lanes. All the turmoil ceases with that one shift. Then you just have one car looking for a fight but no one engaging. It is one of the most satisfying things you can do behind the wheel.

So, those three words spoke to me. They told me to switch lanes. To opt out of the aggressive nature of things and let the aggressors speed on by.

What if I learned how to mentally move over?

I had tried for months to address my anger, but each time I was only explaining myself. I was justifying the need for the anger. I was pleading a case for how wrong other people were and how right I was.

James taught me others weren't the issue. The only thing that mattered was me and how my actions measured up to who I claimed to be. He laid out parameters for behavior that indicated a changed spirit. Doing, not just saying. It's black and white. There isn't a gray area that, provided we explain the transgression, allows us to defend curse words and hateful thoughts.

James says that by yielding, we "plant seeds of peace" (James 3:18). That is something I can get on board with too. I love to plant good seeds.

It was a coolish day in early summer when I watched the rain pour down on the already saturated grass just outside the living room window. The last few months, I had converted the pile of spiral notebooks into something that was beginning to look a lot like a book. It was long enough to be a book. It had a beginning and an end, just like a book. Sometimes I called it a book. It was more of a book than any other compilation of writing I had put together before it.

But something was wrong. For reasons I couldn't define, something wasn't sitting right in my soul. What was I missing?

I stared at the stack of pages, wondering why I had been led to type any of those words. God had brought me through the darkest point in my life and, in the same effort, encouraged me to document it. But why?

I had no business writing about God. I had spent most of my adult life on the threshold of the church, refusing to address or accept large parts of my faith because they made me uncomfortable. There were better people to write things about God out there. People who had never wandered. People who were biblically educated. People whose thoughts were backed up by theology degrees and years of studying. People who didn't drink wine and never slipped in the language department.

I started to reread the pages, curious whether my restlessness came from something within the text—something missing, something I had done wrong, something that proved the inadequacy I felt.

As I read through the pages of my manuscript, I noticed I kept disrupting the story line to address what felt like a third-party reader—a reader who wanted explanations, facts, and a defense of my beliefs. I had inserted verses I thought could prove my points—words intended to protect me. I had reduced my Bible, my favorite book, to reference material, rather than the Living Word I knew it was.

All this was intended as armor to protect me from the third-party critics I imagined would pick my story apart. They were people who didn't believe in God and wouldn't hang with the notion of the Holy Spirit. Others of them wouldn't think I had the skills necessary to tell such a story. They would say I needed to attend seminary or clock more hours in a church pew before writing a story about God.

When I prayed about it, my mind kept flipping back to James and the yielding work I'd addressed with my anger. Had I gotten that wrong? I opened my Bible to the book of James and reread it, noting the areas I'd highlighted while I'd been working through my firebomb of a temper. "Selfish ambition" and "yield" jumped off the page at me.

Now, I'm not super ambitious. In fact, I'm not ambitious at all. Or maybe I'm not ambitious in the same way I usually think of ambition. I picture ambitious people as goal setters. People who are deeply committed to achieving something. People who got better test grades than me in high school and then went on to better colleges than me and then got higher-powered jobs than I did.

I liked to pull weeds and plant vegetables. I was cool with staying home. I liked solitude. I hated competition. It was all part of a master design on my part to self-preserve, to shelter myself from things I saw as dangerous, like criticism or judgment. That was my ambition. So, I guess I *did* have ambition, and it had to do with myself.

Now I had something to work with.

What was number one for me—doing what God wanted or preserving myself? The answer was that I was trying to do both. I wanted to do what God wanted but protect myself in the process. I wanted to shield myself. And by doing so, I wasn't surrendering the whole process to God.

James told me I was supposed to yield to each and every one of those critics. I was supposed to yield the selfish ambition that sought to protect me with words. In yielding that, I could, in turn, yield to my critics. Then my loyalty, as James put it, would no longer be divided between God and the world, and my voice as a writer and as a person would no longer be split, either.

I looked up from my Bible and studied the little sign that hangs in my kitchen, above our calendar. "Let your light shine," it says. The sign reminded me of a discussion I'd had earlier that week with a treasured mentor. She had read parts of the book and could tell I struggled to tell the story to two perceived audiences.

"Who are you writing this for?" she asked with wise eyes.

I knew who God wanted me to write this story for. It was not for my critics. It was for hearts like mine. Hearts rooted in belief, even when God felt far away. Hearts that knew, deep in their core, that no amount of wandering could separate anyone from a love as big as His. It was for the souls that searched for those goose-bump moments when, even though they felt completely alone, they knew they were anything but that. It was for the eyes and hearts that jumped at the realization of the tiny miracles happening on all sides when we were willing to slow down and pay enough attention to find them—the miracles of perfectly timed scriptures; of ancient stories still applicable all these years later; of new relationships and lifelong friends; of faithful family members endlessly committed to sustaining hope; of the promise that comes from new growth, whether it happens in the middle of a flooded garden, a tattered barn, or a brand-new church pew. This was a story for people who loved hope and knew Jesus was the source of the greatest hope of all.

Critics would critique, but I decided I was going to yield out of that so I could tell, without the distraction of explaining, the story that did all of those things for me. I wanted to let the light of the story shine, rather than let my concern for critics put it under a bowl. I wanted it up on a stand, giving light to everyone in the house, just as Matthew 5 talks about.

I grabbed my computer and deleted every last word of armor. Every statement that came from a place of self-preservation. I surrendered each line.

When I was done, new words started pouring back through me, filling each and every gap that remained. Finally, the whole story, word for word, flowed, and the restlessness in my soul ceased.

I sat back in my chair, ready to soak up what I thought would be the glow of accomplishment at a finished manuscript, but no such glow came. Instead, one final scene dropped into my mind, begging to be included. It was a scene I had forgotten to such an extent that, as it crept back into my consciousness, I wasn't sure it was real. Had it happened, or was it a dream?

The fog of a memory kept pushing at the edges of my mind—a memory rooted in the weeks and months that followed our decision to purchase this home. A feeling deep in my soul that had persisted through those days.

Now, I can be forgetful in my own way. I forget eggs at the grocery store. I forget to write down dentist appointments. I forget birthdays.

But even I don't forget stuff like this. Still, I had.

I tried to toss it out of my mind, to politely excuse it from my creative process. But it stayed. It stayed in that gentle yet firm way that confirmed its truth and its origin.

Goose bumps covered my arms, and I felt myself scrambling for a slew of excuses that would permit me to draw the line of remembrance right there. I didn't want to claim this new realization, and I certainly didn't want to process what it meant. I did not want to write it down, nor did I wish to share it with anyone else. The book was done. Adding more to it would be complicated. Never mind the fact that I could barely explain this new piece to myself.

Could my obedience just stop here? I had surrendered in a big way by deleting half the book already, after all.

But as I sat there, processing things, I recognized God had prepared me for dealing with this final piece of the story. I reflected on how, with His guidance, I had learned to follow my nudges. How I had trusted Him as I selected a church and joined the small group. How He had worked with me on my fear and my yielding. I could process this new piece, and I would not do so alone.

So many questions and thoughts circulated, and I knew that a few months earlier, I would have backed out to regroup. But I now knew my scattered brain was just a scattered brain without God. When thoughts poured down like rain on all sides of me, He picked up the pieces and sculpted them into something that made sense to me. I just had to return to Him.

Suddenly I knew I needed to pray. I looked outside and noticed the rain had stopped.

I decided to take a walk.

I set off down the hill, surveying the scene with the same appreciation I always do. The trees glistened with a few remaining drops of rain, and the sun beamed through the cracks in the branches of the oak trees.

I thought back to the first day we had come here to look at this property. It was love at first sight. I desperately wanted this place to be our home. We had made an offer on the house the following day.

Three other offers came in behind ours, and the stress of wondering if our offer would make the cut made me restless.

I had called my mom while we waited to hear if the deal would go through. I had been eager to tell her about the majestic place I had found to raise Ruth. I told her about the hills, the creek, the river, and the trees. It was everything I had ever wanted in a home.

Then she stole my thunder by asking, "Have you prayed?"

I had looked up at the sky, annoyed. Why did she always have to overshadow my moments with prayer talk? Why couldn't she be happy and excited without bringing prayer into it *every single time*?

"Of course I prayed," I replied, shifting my weight under the pressure of the question.

The truth was that I *had* prayed. But it was rare for me to pray about anything at that time in my life. I asked for things and never expected anything other than action. Responses, after all, involved being led, and I wasn't about that.

This situation hadn't been any different. I just wanted help making the sale happen. I wanted the buyers to pick ours over the other offers. I wanted everything to fall into place. I did not want God to weigh in on the yes or no of it. I wanted Him to help me make it happen.

Instead of the silent response I had grown

accustomed to, I was shocked when my prayer seemed to be answered with a strong and heavy, almost audible, *no*.

I immediately started back-peddling. I wanted to flip myself in reverse and take the prayer back. I did not want the no. I wanted the house. I wanted the land. I wanted the place that was a dream come true. I wanted to return the no back from whence it came.

Then I thought that if the no really came from God, He could stop the sale from going through. He could make the buyers deny our offer or make something go wrong in some other part of the negotiations.

But God did not stop the sale. It all went through, and at each step, I felt increasingly perplexed. The burden of the no was so heavy, it tormented me. It would have been easier if God had shut it down instead of making me scramble to figure out, with all certainty, that it was Him saying no in my heart. I wasn't ready to claim that voice with enough conviction to walk away from my dream house.

By this point in my walk, I had reached the barn and stopped to scratch Shadow's golden muzzle, contemplating the weight of this memory of the no and what it signified. I had spent months denying the no I kept hearing. I had tried to explain it away. I'd called it nothing more than moving jitters.

I felt the no as I signed the papers on closing day, and again when the moving truck showed up in our new driveway. I heard it as I unpacked each box, and I tried to ignore it, treating it like a cough or a runny nose—a strange and annoying thing that would eventually clear up over time. But it stayed.

At one point I tried to identify the reason for the no and appease it. My first theory was that God wanted us to stay where we were, near the church we had been regularly attending. That church was a sweet little spot a few miles down the road from our house at the time, with a pastor whose clever and relatable sermons beckoned us to its doorstep week after week. *Yes,* I had thought to myself. The no is about Pastor Mark. We aren't supposed to move away from this church.

Well, we could commute, I decided, tossing the idea to God for approval. We could move to the new house and drive an hour to that church every single Sunday. If I promised to do that, would the no go away?

It did not, and a few weeks later, the no was still in my heart when I heard the news that Pastor Mark had been transferred to Shreveport, five hours away. That's when I knew the no had nothing to do with him. Even God knew we couldn't commute to a church in Shreveport.

When the church proved not to be the source of the no, I theorized it was about finances. Was it managing two mortgages? Were we being careless? If we could sell the other house, then maybe God would stop with the no business. But even as I signed the papers to accept an offer on the other house, I could still feel the weight of the no.

—•—

I stopped walking when I got to the top of the hill.

As I stared down at the two graves below my feet, I slowly realized something: The no only went away when the water showed up. The no stopped the day of the flood.

What's more, the same voice that had brought the no was the same strong, unmistakable nudging voice I'd heard within my heart since I began seeking God again. It was the same voice that had led me through every step of healing from that point forward. It was the same voice I now knew and relied upon every hour of every day.

I sat down on the grass that blanketed the place where Jack and Grady rested and stared up at the sky.

It was all Him.

Tears welled up in my eyes as the moment closed in on me. This humbling moment was God showing me in the most certain of terms exactly who He was.

I thought back to the gentle way I'd been reminded of the no. It was just like the way I introduced Ruth to new things. Not rushing her. Not forcing anything. Wanting her to be prepared for new challenges as she was confronted with them.

I pictured myself transitioning Ruth to her crib. I would rock her to sleep and then tiptoe over to her bed, still bouncing her. I would ease her tiny body onto the soft mattress and rest my hand firmly on her back. I would stay there until her breathing told me she was fast asleep. Each new step, as I did less, proved effortless because the preparation had made her feel secure. Soon she could fall asleep alone, knowing she was safe in her room and that I was near, even though she couldn't see me.

I weaned her from my room and my arms because I knew it was an important first step toward her independence. I knew there would be times she would struggle with it, but it was something she had to be able to do. Because I loved her, I did it in a way that built her confidence for the transition.

That was exactly how it felt for me to be reminded by God of the no.

Because He loves me so much and knows me so well, He waited until I was prepared for it. In the same way I slowly transitioned Ruth to a crib, He slowly transitioned me through my healing. Through that process, I developed the ability to understand it. He didn't thrust it on me. He didn't smack me in the heart with it. Instead, He rocked me through it and then placed me inside the memory of it, His hand resting firmly on my back.

That is who God is.

In this moment of Him revealing Himself to me in such a soft and beautiful way, I couldn't help but think of my buddy, the prophet Elijah, and understand in all certainty what he meant when he said God was not in the mighty windstorm, nor the fire, nor the earthquake. No, God beckoned Elijah out of his cave with a gentle whisper, a whisper I now knew too and could pick out above any other noise.

I twirled a long strand of grass in my fingers, my mind wandering back to the no. Was the no God's way of putting His foot down on my behalf? Had He been trying to stop me from something He knew I couldn't handle? Had He been saying, *No, that would be too much*? I thought back to my anger about the promise in Jeremiah and wondered if this house had not been God's plan for me at all. Could I have avoided all the pain the flood caused if I had been obedient? What would things have looked like today if I had listened?

The moment my mind began to take flight with that possibility, I recognized that when I chased after those thoughts and feelings, I went there alone. I could feel that in my soul. After taking this whole journey with God, I could discern when He wanted me to work harder to understand things and when He wanted me to walk away from them. The "what ifs" of the no don't matter to God.

The truth is that I will never know what would have happened if I had listened. I can't travel down a road I didn't choose to take.

I also know it is no longer important, and understanding how unimportant it is reveals something else I needed to learn about God: God doesn't dwell in the past. He is not vindictive and doesn't keep score. He was using this to show me that.

Through that, I came to understand it was time

for me to release the notion that I was a second-rate Christian. That I didn't measure up to the people who had never stumbled or fallen. That those who had lived lifetimes of trust and obedience were somehow superior to me in His eyes.

Because that is simply not true. It's actually nonsense. God was not looking behind me. He simply wanted me to turn and face Him. He wanted me to pivot from how I used to make decisions toward how I intend to make them moving forward. He wanted my commitment to trust and obey.

It was a sunny Wednesday morning when I pulled into the parking lot of the church and saw two vans from visiting, out-of-state congregations—missions crews coming to help as we continued to restore our community from the flood. They were still committed to our revival nearly a year later.

I was surprised by the tears that filled my eyes at the sight of the pink uppercase letters that lined the windows along the back of the vehicle. "WE LOVE YOU, BATON ROUGE," they said.

"We can feel it," I whispered under my breath with a smile.

I tried to compose myself as I headed into church, chasing Ruth up the ramp as she hurried to find her treasured friends in the basement below. I settled her there and then headed into the small space where our little group was meeting to study the book of Esther. A fitting choice.

As everyone came in and sat down, I opened my book and smiled at the first question for the day: "What are you afraid of?" I still had a list, but these days that list felt a whole lot shorter, and I felt a whole lot lighter than ever before.

For two hours, we did the same thing we did every week. We laughed. We studied the Word. We prayed. We built each other up for whatever battles we would face in the week ahead. Some days we tackled toddlers and tantrums. On others, we tackled tragedy and loss.

In that moment I reflected on how I spent my entire adult life building up an armor within myself against women I didn't know. I distrusted them and their motives. I'd been burned too many times by females. I'd built up a solid group of women in my life with whom I felt safe, ones who had undergone an intense vetting process over months and years. I had seen no need to expose myself to an unknown and unchecked group of females.

Looking at these women in my life now and the impact each one of them has had not just on my healing but on the general well-being of my soul, I have a new appreciation for trusting God more than I trust myself. Sometimes God's biggest miracles happen when He connects His people. Sometimes the greatest work is completed through the relationships He forges.

That afternoon as I drove us home, the summer sun shone down on the trees, which had exploded with vibrant green color in true South Louisiana fashion. The magnolias were in full bloom, and giant white flowers covered their towering emerald frames.

I crossed the bridge over the Amite River, whose water was well within its banks. Its beautiful white sandy beaches, lined with cypress trees draped in Spanish moss, were fully exposed once again.

A few miles south of my house, I got stopped on the road while an eighteen-wheeler backed a load of sheetrock and insulation down a driveway. I looked up and noticed the debris pile at the house across the street had finally been picked up. The family had planted sunflower seeds in its place. It was a funny sight to see the tiny stalks popping through shards of glass, pieces of porcelain, and chips of wood that remained on the torn-up and disheveled lawn. The little flowers were smaller than normal, stunted from their less-than-ideal growing conditions, but no less uplifting.

The truck made its way off the road, and we were given the right of way to keep rolling.

Ten minutes later, I pulled into my driveway and hopped out to get the mail. As I walked back to the car, I sifted through the pile of catalogs and coupons and smiled as my fingers came to rest on a large manila envelope at the bottom of the stack. A new order of seeds.

The following evening, Mynde and I stood in my kitchen, taking in the chaos that had ensued in the once-clean space. Our goal for the night had been simple and easy, yet our two well-intentioned husbands had taken *simple* to mean *culinary exploration*. They'd strewn pots and pans everywhere, and two different kinds of sauces simmered on the stove. Half-chopped vegetables covered four cutting boards. It would all have seemed wonderful if it wasn't the same kitchen I'd spent hours cleaning earlier that day.

I looked at Mynde and saw her shaking her head, no doubt wondering how the dots of *simple* and *easy* had gotten disconnected.

"Let's go down to the barn," I said, as if replying to her thoughts.

She nodded in agreement. We loved walking down there in the evening, letting the kids expend their last bits of energy down the bends of the little dirt road.

As we stepped out onto the porch, Mynde slipped her freshly manicured feet out of her sandals and tugged on a pair of mud boots. I laughed.

"What?" she asked. "I know I can't go anywhere with you without my mud boots on."

The long and winding path echoed with the kids'

giggles as the three of them ran down it, full speed ahead, stopping occasionally to peek from behind the trees that lined its path. The dogs ran alongside them, delighting in the moment.

When we reached the barn, we took a seat on the swing and rocked slowly, watching the kids as they wrestled with giant armfuls of hay to feed to Shadow and Mesquite, who stood with their heads peeking over their stall doors.

The sun was setting just right, and it sparkled through the trees onto the hill just behind the barn. I looked over at Mynde and saw tears welling up in her eyes as she surveyed the scene.

"Aww, bud," I said. "It feels good down here, doesn't it?"

I couldn't help but tear up at the sight of this friend who was so moved by my restoration that it made her cry.

"I love you," I said, looking at her and meaning it.

I looked around us. Markers and painting supplies covered the small table in the center of the barn. The air smelled like pine shavings and freshly cut hay. I rubbed the swing with my hand and remembered Brad hoisting it up in the rafters that cool spring day. I turned my gaze to the woods and could still see my dad there, hauling my stuff out, trip after trip, in the hot August heat. I glanced at the halters hanging on the hooks and smiled at the thought of my mom, flying in from Boston and giving me two new halters, two new lead ropes, and so much more. She was encouraging me to love again and, more importantly, to trust again.

As the silence of that moment lifted, it felt like the weight of the year behind us went with it. It no longer needed our words. All of the pain and anguish had been replaced with the calming notion of peace.

At just the right moment, Mynde broke the silence. "Now we just need to figure out what to do with our husbands..."

I laughed at the lightness of it.

"They don't listen, do they?" I asked, tugging at the tear on the side of my weathered boots and looking up with a grin.

I sat back and gazed at the huge oak tree set back from the barn, just past the wood line. Its limbs stretched farther than I could see.

"But you know," I continued, "I realized the other day that nothing ever made me want to listen better or follow instructions more than being loved in spite of a giant mess I'd created from not doing either one of those things very well. So I think I'm going to walk up that hill, take a look at that messy kitchen, and hug Brad tighter than he deserves in this moment."

I paused, then grinned.

"And then I'm going to help him while he cleans it up," I finished.

Mynde laughed. "I love it. Where'd you get that idea from?"

"Jesus," I said. "And some Jeremiah."

"You're still reading Jeremiah?" Her face erupted with a smile.

"Tessa and I were loving Jeremiah so much the other day," I said, "that we bought a book *about* the book. I don't know what to say. Every time that I think I'm done with him, He"—I paused, pointing upward—"keeps calling me back for more. Plus, Jeremiah is super wordy and disorganized, and that's kind of my thing."

As we laughed, I could feel my grandfather's smile in every inch of my face, certain that if our photos were aligned in that moment, our features would be aligned too. I wasn't hiding any discontentment. I was happy.

The lyrics of "Trust and Obey" began to run in my mind.

Of course Grandy loved that song, I thought. *How could he not?*

Epilogue

I put Ruth down for her nap, grab the new collection of seeds, and head out to the garden. The little space is now outlined by a beautiful cedar fence, Brad's solution to the growing issue of nighttime critters sneaking in and eating my plants.

The gate creaks as I open it, and my eyes light up at the spectacular display of color and growth that greets me.

To my left stands a beautiful lemon tree covered in shiny, green leaves and a few plump and promising fruit buds. I can still see in my mind the sweet face of the teenaged girl who gave it to me with tear-filled eyes in the days following the flood. She had been a devoted caregiver for Jack and Grady, and despite her grief over their deaths, she was determined to show me compassion through the gesture of this gift. Her mother told me the young girl had spent her own hard-earned money on the tree and had been intentional to select one bearing fruit.

A few feet away sits a bright blue hydrangea. I brought it home and planted it shortly after my great-aunt passed away. Its blooms bring me back to the doorstep of her home on Martha's Vineyard. It's my hope that whenever I see that little shrub, it will encourage me to let the witness of her deeds guide me and my priorities.

A few small boxwoods seemed a fitting addition to the mix of shrubs and perennials, and I take a deep breath as I round the corner toward their spot. I don't ever want to forget the smell or the feeling of home those tiny evergreens bring to me. And I never want to lose touch with the little girl within me who loves Scripture and believes in a God who is as big as He really is.

Across the way, an aloe plant soaks up the sun's rays in a terra cotta pot. It was a gift from my friend Amy. We met at the church I thought was too big, in the group I thought was too intimidating. I find it perfect that a person who soothes my soul gave me a plant that is soothing by nature.

Behind the aloe stands a sad-looking glass terrarium filled with succulents. It was my attempt to re-create something Tessa and I found on Pinterest, but it looks more like a kindergarten craft project. I laugh, looking at it, as it carries a funny symbolism all its own. Tessa and I know things don't always go as planned. Our friendship was born when things were very much not going as planned. But we never let that stop us from trying. I am eternally grateful for a friend and a neighbor who knows as well as I do that all that matters is that we remember to bow down and then look up.

In the back of the garden are two large hibiscus trees that bloom constantly in three different colors, a gift from my mother-in-law, one of the most generous hearts I know. Between them stands a forsythia bush, just like the ones my mother tends at our home in Massachusetts. Below all of them stretches a tenacious patch of strawberries, just like the one my dad and I had growing up. And then there is the grapefruit tree my father-in-law contributed to my growing orchard the year before. Looking at all of them, I know how important and unique a parent's love is.

Two gorgeous muscadine vines line the back of the garden. Brad gave them to me for Valentine's Day the year before the flood. They survived and came back the following spring, more fruitful than the year before. They remind me of our marriage, weathering storms and displaying beautiful growth with each new year.

In the center of the space, a giant flower garden spills over with color. I would trim it back, but it's not mine to trim. That space belongs to my sweet little girl. Every time I look at it, I find myself encouraged by her relentless optimism. She's been through a lot in her short life, but she still thinks the world is inherently beautiful, and she continues to have faith in new growth and good seeds.

I look around my garden and see how much the flood has changed it. It's nothing like it was before the water rose and washed every bit of our hard work away.

It's better.

The garden that stood here before the flood was so pragmatic. Every season, I made charts and planned for plants with predictable growth patterns and obvious use. Nothing was ever *just planted*.

I was kind of the same way as a person. I spent my whole life engaged in projects and commitments with obvious outcomes. I did things that produced results I could quantify. I didn't plant things just to smell them or see them. I didn't write just to write. I rarely sat down, and I never searched for things in silence. But now a bench takes up a large portion of my garden, reminding me that stillness is just as important as motion and that not everything has to have a measurable outcome.

Perhaps the most beautiful thing of all is that somewhere in that transformation, I opened my garden, and myself, to the contributions of others. They brought growth and color and new dimension not just to my plot, but to my soul. Alone, my garden was a functional space that served a purpose, but it was flat. With the help and gifts of other people, the space has come alive with depth, texture, and hues it wouldn't have otherwise known.

I grin as I bend over and cut the string that has supported my apple tree since last August. The tree doesn't stand as straight as it did before the flood, but I no longer see a problem in its slight bend. That bend is a reminder of changes that took place here. Its roots ensure its growth is strong and its blossoms are fruitful.

Then I turn and walk over to the freshly tilled patch of soil I prepared yesterday. I take four new bags of flower seeds, rip the tops off, and scatter them. I smile, embracing the fact that I don't need to know or control the outcome of their growth. They are good seeds being planted in good soil. Whatever comes of them will be good too.

Acknowledgments

God, thank You for keeping your arms wide open, even for Your most stubborn children. Your plans and Your promises are so very beautiful.

Jesus, thank You for coming to this world to teach me how to live, how to love, and how to suffer with purpose.

Holy Spirit, thank You for filling me up, moving my mountain, and leading me through each word of this book.

Dad, thank you for raising me with tenacity and a love for planting seeds. Thank you for meeting me in my muddiest places and for pulling me out of them. And thank you, again, for always checking my closet for monsters.

Mom, thank you for always asking me if I prayed, even when you knew I hadn't. Thank you for always giving me Bibles, even when you knew I wasn't reading them. Thank you for always seeing the best in me, even when I had a hard time seeing the best in myself.

Brad, thank you for being with me through sunny days and stormy weather. Thank you for supporting every dream I have, even when they are not your own. I am loving you always, in every minute of every day.

Ruth, thank you for always watching me from the back seat of the car. Thank you for your relentless optimism. Thank you for sharing my love for new growth and packets of seeds.

Greg, thank you for clever cards, for thoughtful gifts, and for sounding exactly like Grandy when you sing a hymn. I am grateful to be your little sister.

Ben, I needed your truck in my driveway last fall. Thank you for realizing that and for coming, even though it took sixteen hundred miles to get here. You have always been a rock for me, no matter where you are.

William Emerson Gilmour, thank you for showing me how to trust and obey. Thank you for continuing to love the sky and insisting that there was beauty in airplanes. You dazzled me in every moment of our time together. I hope I am dazzling you right now in some small way too.

Marjorie Hancock Phillips, thank you for being such a beautiful example of faithful obedience in my life. Thank you for reminding me of my roots when I wasn't sure if I still had them in me. Every time I see blue hydrangeas, I will think of you and ask myself if I am living up to your standards of love and service to others.

To my family and friends, near and far: I was in a tug-of-war between hope and hopelessness. Thanks to your kindness and generosity, hope won.

Tommy and Beverly, I am grateful for each plant you have brought me for my garden, for cypress swings hung in my barn, and for the gift of in-laws like you.

Shirley Schofield, thank you for being a living example of Christlike love in the lives of those around you. Whether I was a little girl baking cookies in your home, a teenager being fed by you at summer camp, or an adult woman in the midst of a tragedy, you have been a witness to me, and I will not forget it.

Kaity and Kevin Cimo, I am so grateful for two friends whose response to every single crazy scheme I have is, "That's an awesome idea. How can we help?" Kev, you have gone above and beyond by creating the beautiful cover for my book. Every time I look at it, I am reminded of my two endlessly encouraging and talented friends who always believe in and support my ideas.

Amanda Guthrie, thank you for loving my stories and inspiring me to tell more of them. You may live far away, but there is a special place for you in my soul.

Mynde Breed, thank you for laughing at my jokes even when they aren't that funny, for loving my cooking even when it's not that good, and for buying a pair of mud boots because you know life with me can be muddy.

Matt Breed, the world would be a better place if everyone had a friend as loyal as you. You come through for our family in our muddiest and messiest times. Thank you for jumping in and not standing on the sidelines when things get rough.

Tessa Dempre, you share my appreciation for trash day, my taste for wine, my curiosity for the Bible, and my love for Jesus. I am so grateful you are my neighbor and my friend.

Amy Book, thank you for loving me before you knew me, for loving this book before you read it, and for believing in my ability to get to this point before I believed it myself. I prayed for courage, and God responded by giving me the gift of your beautiful friendship.

Christianne Squires, when I prayed for a person to help me usher this book into this world, I couldn't have imagined a more perfect person than you. You have woven love into each paragraph of its pages. You have asked me questions that led to my spiritual growth, not just my growth as a writer. You gave me confidence that I can tell a good story and that what I created was indeed a book, and I needed to hear both of those things. You have been instrumental in making this process one I can complete. Your work and your vision are both beautiful. Thank you for being such a prayerful and talented bookwife.

Reverend Pattye Hewitt, thank you for teaching me "The Danger of Anger." Your messages always seem to speak right to my soul.

Reverend Ann Trousdale, your comments encouraged me to embrace my true voice, and in doing so,

I found my purpose. I am grateful for your time and your wisdom.

Cherri Johnson, thank you for encouraging me to let go of the things that I was never intended to hold on to. It gave me the freedom to break free and get to my intended destination.

To my sweet friends in CORE, you ladies center me, you restore me, and you encourage me. Thank you for having open hearts and open doors.

First United Methodist Church of Baton Rouge, thank you for being big on hope and small when it matters. I am so grateful I finally mustered the courage to step all the way across your threshold.

Trinitarian Congregational Church, your boxwoods may be gone, but I will always feel at home within your walls. Thank you for filling up my little soul with a love and wonder for Jesus. You plant good seeds.

Made in the USA
Lexington, KY
09 December 2017